ROGUE NATION

ROGUE NATION

Dispatches from Australia's populist uprisings and outsider politics

ROYCE KURMELOVS

hachette
AUSTRALIA

Quote from *Off the Rails: The Pauline Hanson Trip* by Margo Kingston, Allen & Unwin, Sydney, Copyright © Margo Kingston 1999.

hachette
AUSTRALIA

Published in Australia and New Zealand in 2017
by Hachette Australia
(an imprint of Hachette Australia Pty Limited)
Level 17, 207 Kent Street, Sydney NSW 2000
www.hachette.com.au

10 9 8 7 6 5 4 3 2 1

Copyright © Royce Kurmelovs 2017

A catalogue record for this book is available from the National Library of Australia

ISBN: 978 0 7336 3924 1 (paperback)

Cover design by Luke Causby, Blue Cork
Cover photographs courtesy of Newspix (NP1202463/Kym Smith, NP148199/Toby Zerna, NP1172417/ Kym Smith, NP1161344/Chris Kidd)
Author photo courtesy of Jonathan van der Knaap
Typeset in Sabon LT by Kirby Jones
Printed and bound in Australia by McPherson's Printing Group

MIX
Paper from responsible sources
FSC® C001695

The paper this book is printed on is certified against the Forest Stewardship Council® Standards. McPherson's Printing Group holds FSC® chain of custody certification SA-COC-005379. FSC® promotes environmentally responsible, socially beneficial and economically viable management of the world's forests.

Contents

Preface

The modern Australian politician should be of the people, but not one of them. They should enjoy beer, but never be seen falling down drunk. They should swear in private with their friends and allies, but not in public and never at their enemies. They should speak plainly. They should be charismatic. They should know how to give a speech to a room full of people who love them, and how to give a speech to a room full of people who hate them. No matter what, they should never react angrily to scrutiny, or heckling, or personal attacks. They should know poetry and literature, but only talk about these things in private, otherwise they will be considered weak.

An Australian politician should be tough. They should respect sportspeople and follow a team. On grand final day, they should watch with the nation and know the result. They should not back down to bullies. They should always say what they feel, but show restraint in what they say. They must have a considered opinion on all things, or be willing to bluff convincingly. They should answer direct questions, no matter how painful. A politician should never lie, unless it is in the national interest, or a time of national emergency, and then they should lie well, so people can respect them for it.

A politician should be intelligent, but not superior. They should be educated, but not arrogant. They should be of the land, of the factory, or of a trade. They should know how to work with their hands, and this knowledge should inform their political work. They should work hard and live frugally. They should respect the public purse. They should be successful, but not rich, and if they are they should never advertise it.

A politician should have a family and cherish it, but never deploy it as a political weapon. They should cherish their children and govern with their future in mind. They should cherish their god and live by their beliefs, but never judge those who do not. Australians hate a preacher.

They should respect their leader, respect the process and respect their office. They should read the polls and respond to them, but know when to hold through the flak. They should be comfortable with power and know how to wield it like a scalpel, or a sledgehammer, but should never covet it. They should have vision and show leadership. They should include everyone, but know when to make a decision. They should bend, but never break, no matter how much pressure they are under. They should work to improve the lot of all.

This is the ideal of Australian political leadership; a person who cannot exist, has never existed and probably will never exist. Politicians may be afforded the dignity and authority that comes with public office, but politics is full of well-meaning, respectable people, as prone to dumb mistakes, petty vengeance and arrogant self-delusion as anyone else. Some are stone-cold stupid, with no imagination or passion for anything outside their own limited experience. Some may chafe at the party platform but never break ranks. With nothing to say, some may fall back on campaign slogans or talk in folksy clichés. Under personal threat, some may lie. They may talk big, but never act. They may love to win, at any cost, or have discovered a twisted interpretation of the world and their place within it. Others have simply confused their own naked ambition with talent, or had someone else confuse their naked ambition with talent.

With enough time, many politicians can make peace with their flaws and may even overcome them, putting them to work as something personal and unique. Sometimes they may have an opportunity to do some good in a city like Canberra where party lines are being erased and it feels like everyone has become a free agent. Sometimes they may even make something out of that opportunity.

Everyone, eventually, falls short. Every single one. And when powerful people start to look ordinary, those who vote for them start to think that ordinary people might do a better job. Break the illusion enough times and people start to cast around for alternatives.

This is a book about those alternatives. It is not a political polemic or a sociological treatise, though it has something to say on both those accounts. This book is a snapshot of a time when the rules of the game seemed to be changing, when Pauline Hanson had returned despite the odds and people were grappling with what it meant.

In 2016, I went to work as media advisor to Senator Nick Xenophon for five months. I left after being given an opportunity to write a book about what happened after the mining boom. Around that time, various media outlets asked me to write about US President Donald Trump and whether what happened in the United States could happen in Australia. People wanted to know about Pauline Hanson. People wanted to know about populism. People wanted to know about the lives of poor and working-class people, and whatever it was they were thinking.

I didn't end up writing those stories. Instead I was offered the chance to put together this book as a field report on the health of our democracy, asking why politics seemed to be unable to see the barbarians coming until they were storming the gate. In doing so I had to revisit my brief time in politics – a hazy montage of memories – and work out what I had learned. Then I had to build on it.

The more I thought about it, the more I came to understand I had gone in cynical and I had come out the other side still cynical, but in a different way. Politics, I learned, is a place where the full range of human potential is on display, every day. There are good, decent people in there doing their best, and there are ruthless, calculating psychopaths who don't care at all.

All, I learned, are prisoners of their circumstances and the certainties of their worldview.

Nothing encapsulated this message more than the unexpected return of One Nation. In a lot of ways, Hanson was the political story of the decade, though as far as I was concerned, Pauline Hanson was the least interesting thing about Pauline Hanson. She was someone who preyed on the hopes and frustrations of working-class and country people. Too much ink has been spilled on taking her apart.

I was more interested in the environment around her. I wanted to know *why*. Why now? Who voted for Pauline? And what had happened to us, and to the rest of the world, when fear-mongers and conspiracy nuts were suddenly put in charge of nuclear codes and the national budget?

To answer these questions, I set out with my pen and pad to outline the lives and careers of some of those political leaders Australians had chosen from outside the major political parties to represent them and, where possible, to sketch the people who had voted for them, or those who hadn't. In doing so, I wanted to piece together what had happened in order to understand this 'populist moment', although I did not want to write it from the perspective of the major parties, be they blue or red or green. Instead, my book would be told from the perspective of the rogues and the strays who are now sitting in parliament.

This is also a book I never intended to write. I kept no special notebook during my time in politics, though sometimes I would threaten Nick Xenophon with the idea that one day I would write his biography. The stories and observations I share from this time are memories fleshed out as best I can, aided by documents, records, news articles, press releases and conversations with the people I worked alongside, and those I met along the way. A few chapters have been the product of previous journalism, while the rest has been put together by working the phones and heading out on the road, because politics, I still believe somewhat earnestly, is more than the process of passing a bill. It is something that happens *out there*, on the street corners, in the coffee shops and fields, even in your living room. Power is a cooperative relationship. Parliament may give, and parliament may take, but it's the people living on the other side of those decisions – the powerless – who define what is acceptable.

So, I figured, if I wanted to understand something like Pauline Hanson with any real clarity, if I wanted to know what the hell happened *out there*, I had to be out there with the rest of them.

'There's something about being surrounded by
white boys in blue suits that just crushes my libido.'

Senate staffer on the environment of
Parliament House, 2017

Chapter 1

CANBERRA'S RELIGION HAS ANGRY GODS

It was about three in the afternoon when we decided we needed a drink.

We had made our way down to the staff cafeteria through the winding corridors of Parliament House in Canberra, the seat of Australian democracy. An eerie silence had settled over the building and the whole place fell still.

'It's a little bit like the apocalypse,' Jono said.

We were seated in the couch section, over towards the back, and a chef in the cafeteria offered to get us some beer from a fridge in another room. While we waited, we tried to make sense of what had just happened.

Jono and I had been working up in Senate suite S1.56 while the votes were being counted. We had turned up to work at seven that morning, maybe a little earlier, and switched on the television, along with the whole world, to watch the final crescendo of a thundering presidential campaign, to find out what the American people would decide.

For months a sense of denial had knocked about the world of politics. Trump had no chance, the thinking had gone. He was crazy, crooked and vile. Hillary wasn't perfect, but she was safe, she was experienced and she knew what she was doing. It was only when the results started to roll in that the collective delusion lifted and the realisation dawned that it was Hillary who had lost. It was Trump for President 2017.

Rome burned, and all its allies could do was watch. Donald J. Trump might not have been an Australian president, but the very fact he had climbed his way out of Trump Tower to take control of the biggest economy, military and nuclear arsenal in the world suddenly marked a dramatic shift in what was possible. Every rule of the game seemed to have been redefined.

Jono belonged to that group who had never really believed that Trump had a chance. He was Nick Xenophon's legislative advisor, a lawyer and a canny tactician with a sunny smile from a working-class family in small-town Burnie, Tasmania. As a kid he had visited Parliament House and rolled down its green hills. Something in that grass must have got under his skin, because from that moment on, all he had wanted was to work in the Big House.

He got his chance with former senator Ricky Muir, an average guy pulled off the street and elevated to parliament by sheer dumb luck. In his job interview Jono told Muir that he had never really worked in politics, but he would work hard if given the chance. Muir liked his honesty and agreed to give him his shot. Together, they got about two years out of it before the major parties ended their streak by rewriting the rules so an unknown quantity like Muir would never be allowed to take office again.

The night of the 2016 federal election, Muir lost and Jono wandered through Parliament House, thinking those were going to be his last hours, until Nick Xenophon floated the idea that Jono might want to come to work for him.

The other camp – those who saw Trump coming a mile off – was represented by Philip Dorling, a bespectacled, jaded ex-Fairfax journalist who had been around Canberra longer than anyone could remember. He had a $100 bottle of wine riding on the outcome of the US election with a staffer from another office, and from the moment the count started he closely monitored the result.

'Just look at that map,' Philip said from across the office as the votes piled up. On his computer screen splashed a map showing all the different counties in the United States and which way they had voted. For the most part, California and New York had turned blue for the Democrats. Everything in between was cherry red, bricking up the centre of the country and dividing the world's last remaining superpower right down the middle.

At that point, the count was only halfway, so I asked whether he thought Hillary still had a chance.

'It's over,' he said. 'Just take a look. There's no coming back from that. You just don't want to believe it.'

Philip had known Trump was coming, he said, ever since he went on a Defence Force study tour during which he ate crabs along a riverbank in some hick part of the United States near where he was working. The Americans he dined with that day were obese, loud, deeply in debt, with no education and no real future for their kids, he told me. These were the people who voted for Trump. They were good, God-fearing people who didn't care about bad manners; all they heard was Trump talking about how he was going to bring back the good jobs, drain the swamp and make America great again, and they liked it.

It was a line of thinking that made a lot of sense to me. I was a skinny kid from Adelaide's north who had graduated from an under-resourced public school where I once got stomped on the oval by a guy with 'newboys' tattooed across his forearms. The further north you went, the higher the unemployment figure ticked, well above the national average, even as the rest of the country went about its business without a care in the world.

Politics took no real interest in us while I was growing up, and when it did, it talked about the whole region as a problem to be solved, or forgotten, instead of consulted about its future. In the national scheme of things, we were losers. Politics was something the rest of the country did, something we watched briefly on the evening news before they cut to the sport. Not once do I remember a candidate knocking on our front door to ask my family about our views and talk about our problems, and if they had, we would probably have pretended we weren't home anyway.

A few months before I started working for Nick Xenophon, I published a book about my people, who were watching on as the car industry, the backbone of the local economy, shut down. It was a strange book, for both me and the local community. People with my roots don't often become writers or work in media, because it doesn't occur to them that they might, and the stories of people I wrote about don't normally get told in any depth unless some dumb kid leads police on a chase through the outer suburbs.

4

It was, however, a book that had to be written. Politics might not have taken much of an interest in where I grew up, but in that moment politics took away the last best thing the community had left on the basis that the rest of the country was no longer willing to subsidise it. During that time, I saw the confusion, frustration and grief in people's eyes. I listened to them as they wondered aloud about their future, about how they were working two jobs, or no job, and how they worried for the future of their children. And then I wrote it all down in the name of journalism.

It was Australia's American Dream, I had written, and we were about to wake up to the nightmare.

I might not have known that Donald Trump was coming to the United States, but I knew something was happening Down Under. I had seen enough to know that when people start to worry about their future, they start to look for alternatives.

Before I had signed on for a couple of months with Nick Xenophon – or Nick, as he prefers to be called – I was working as a freelance journalist, a stray grinding out copy for any news outlet that would have me. I had covered Reclaim Australia rallies in two states and watched the return of One Nation with a sense of foreboding. Donald Trump was just a local American chapter of a global story, but whatever happened, however it played out, I knew it would come here eventually.

So, when Nick made me an offer to work in his press shop about a month after my book came out, I took it. I had spent the previous four years living cheque-to-cheque, and had become exhausted by the hustle. To top it off, one crisis after another had taken over the lives of my parents. When that happens, and someone offers to help pay your rent for the foreseeable future, you don't say no.

Then there was the sense of adventure: it was an opportunity. Agreeing would mean embedding with the 'feral Senate', that loose band of political rebels who resisted Tony Abbott's hard-wired authoritarian impulse to rewrite the way of Australian social and political life.

These senators, those who existed beyond the ranks of the major parties, were outsiders. A defiant group of contrarians – and occasionally straight-out freaks – who had gradually come to represent those Australians who had been left behind. In turn, they became kingmakers. This group of people were simultaneously riding the same global forces that had delivered Trump to the White House while still largely keeping to the rules of the game.

In among it was One Nation. They were something new-ish, a kind of expeditionary force for the Trump campaign who had clawed their way back from obscurity at the 2016 federal election to secure four Senate seats. In the months afterwards, we watched the situation develop through our daily routines, and, sitting in our office, we came to the understanding that those with the most to lose from the return of One Nation were the independents. Once Trump had gone global, all it would take was one heartfelt lie in a post-fact universe for One Nation to sweep through those areas of the country that were so cynical, so withdrawn, they would turn the whole system on its head for a laugh.

And on US Election Day, One Nation were the only ones celebrating as we walked down to the cafeteria. In their suite, they had popped the cork on a champagne bottle and extended an invitation for everyone to join. We had politely declined.

So, while Philip Dorling ducked out early to collect on his bet, Jono and I went to the cafeteria to take stock.

'This is one of those days we will remember,' Jono said. 'Where were you when Trump was elected? Sitting in the seat of Australian democracy. Some day we'll tell our grandchildren about this moment.'

We clinked our bottles.

'You think it could happen here?' Jono asked after a moment's pause.

'No doubt,' I said. It already was happening here. There was a whole horde of angry people out there in search of a leader. If Canberra's religion was politics, we were sinners in the hands of angry gods.

It was only a question of who, and how long.

Chapter 2

ON CANARIES AND COAL MINES

PAULINE HANSON WAS BORN PAULINE SECCOMBE IN 1954 IN Brisbane, Queensland. She was the fifth child in a family of seven children. From a young age Hanson worked in her father's cafe as a cook and a waitress, and when she got older she helped with the books. At fifteen, she left school just before her first marriage and her first pregnancy with Walter Zagorski, a Polish refugee whose mother had lived through the Holocaust. Later she worked at Woolworths, then in office administration and after that she tended bars on the Sunshine Coast. When she drove, she liked to drive fast.

She was poor, in the early days, with kids to feed and no education, and that's when she learned the value of a dollar. Her first marriage ended when she was twenty-one. During her second marriage, she took the surname of Mark Hanson and together the couple set up a plumbing company. He did the work, she took care of the books, and when that relationship burned down, so did the business.

She did, however, keep the name – the one that would eventually become an iconic Australian brand – and in the ruins of her second marriage, she built a catering service with Morrie Marsden. Together they built a fish-and-chip shop, though she preferred not to call it that. It was a 'seafood takeaway' according to Hanson. Her innovation had been to bring fresh fish to Ipswich, in what was once coal country. Four times a week, always at dawn, she went down to the fish market to buy her stock. She worked fourteen hours a day, six days out of seven.

Then came politics. Government was a growth industry and politics was financially secure, so Hanson tried her hand, first running as a councillor in Ipswich during a time of closing mines and failing businesses. She only served from 1994 to 1995, after a redistribution forced an election, making her the shortest-serving councillor in the region's history since 1860. She hated unions and ran her campaign promising to slash funding to the local library, which would have allowed it to set up a proto-internet, because it was a waste of ratepayers' money. A year after being elected she lost the next election, never having really learned anything about the political process.

After that she scrambled into federal politics on the Liberal Party's ticket with Morrie Marsden as her campaign manager and her first media advisor John Pasquarelli by her side. It was a good fit. Hanson's people were small-business owners. They were local merchants in a working-class region, and they believed in self-reliance above all else. By the time she first made a run at federal politics in 1996, Hanson owned land worth $500000 just outside of Ipswich and an apartment in Brisbane. Under any other circumstances she would have been another grey major-party candidate, another minor captain in the blue army.

Then came the crisis. Hanson penned a letter to the editor of the *Queensland Times* on 6 January 1996, complaining that white deaths in custody were being overlooked and Indigenous people were being 'showered with money'. The editor suggested she might want to reconsider running it, but Hanson insisted that it went to press. These days, it would be held up by party headquarters as a textbook example of why they don't let candidates talk to media.

When he learned of it, John Howard, as leader of the Liberal Party, dropped her from the ticket and banished her from the party, but Hanson leaned in. Out in the community, the region's economy was going to Hell, and Labor were on the out after the mayor, a Labor man, was dethroned by his own people. Chance meant that the words 'Liberal Party' appeared next to her name on the ballot and she rode the outrage to victory on Election Day, carrying 23 per cent of the primary vote in the safest Labor seat in Australia.

No one could believe it. Nothing about it had been planned. It was one of those things that just happened, like childbirth during a meteor shower.

She made a bigger splash with her maiden speech, written by Pasquarelli, and when it hit the newswires, it went around the world for stoking fears that the country would be 'swamped by Asians'. What Hanson wanted was equality, she said, though not the kind of equality they like to talk about on the left. Hanson didn't want to share the wealth, or equal opportunity. She wanted a world where everyone was neglected equally, so as to lift the burden on the working-class Anglo-Saxon male. It has always been race and class with Hanson, never race *or* class.

Years before a wave of populist, nationalist sentiment swept much of the world, Australia did it first, and in that moment Hanson seemed to confirm every stereotype the world had about Australia being the world's trailer park. Asia-based multinationals were so fearful about what her brand of xenophobia would mean for their companies, they had English-speaking officers send regular reports directly to headquarters, keeping them informed about the situation. Even her former mother-in-law was afraid that Hanson might want to deport her, at least according to David Leser's profile in the *Sydney Morning Herald*.

None of which fazed Hanson. She had a knack for flipping the script to evade any uncomfortable questions. It was a tactic she deployed against anyone brash enough to think that a forensic interrogation of the facts was all they needed to cut to the core of Pauline Hanson. Those reporters who had the opportunity to interview her during this time all tell the same war story, the same moment when they pushed too hard on a line of questioning that highlighted some flaw in Hanson's worldview, or understanding of an issue, and especially anything that seemed to suggest she was racist. Right then, Hanson's eyes would zero in on her questioner, and the quiver in her voice that suggested nervousness mixed with fury vanished as she began to interrogate her interviewer.

She would always push back, asking the interviewer why they assumed she was racist. It was impossible to intellectually engage with Hanson's reasoning without offending her, and the reporter, so sure of themselves only a moment before, would stumble while Hanson side-stepped the entire question and went on the offensive.

Two years on, Hanson would be up for re-election, after re-districting forced her to switch seats to Blair. Her new party, One Nation, shared its name with the title of a speech Don Watson had written for Labor prime minister Paul Keating, and she barnstormed the country to spread the word. Hanson criss-crossed the nation speaking to people's desperation, to their naivety, to their resentment and their confusion. She would listen to them in conversation and she would reflect back their fears, whether it was anxiety about Indigenous land rights and migration, or outrage over dole bludgers taking them for a free ride. It was a formula that earned her a blind loyalty. She listened, it was said. The bastards in Canberra didn't.

That's how the Queensland branch of her party won 11 out of 89 seats in Queensland's state parliament during the June 1998 state election, with 23 per cent of the vote.

Only, three and a half months later Hanson herself would be dethroned, losing to a Liberal Party flunkey who got over the line on a preference deal done with Labor. Hanson won the highest number of votes in her seat – more than Liberal, more than Labor – but the preference deal between the majors snuffed her out. It was something she never forgot, and the party faithful couldn't understand. Few members of One Nation had the political literacy to comprehend the why and how of the loss. Even fewer had the interest. The very concept of a preference deal was mind-bending to One Nation and its supporters. When they learned the details, they saw it as further proof that the system was rigged and the biggest enemy was the process itself.

Not that it mattered. Just by being, Hanson reshaped the world around her. She had enough popularity to quietly win some of the local burghers to her side and she marshalled enough support that Howard, never afraid to play the race card, co-opted her platform into the Liberal Party's politics.

Faced with an insurgency, Howard had waged a campaign of scorched earth that ultimately drove One Nation to collapse. Hanson herself did an eleven-week stint in the lock-up for screwing around with the party paperwork, before her conviction was overturned, and the general feeling among the political class then, and now, was that it was a stitch-up. Tony Abbott, the then future Prime Minister of Australia, ex-boxer and the Liberal Party's Rottweiler, had gone too hard and too far on that one, bankrolling a $100 000 fighting fund to send her there for three years. He later apologised to Hanson.

It was also the biggest favour anyone could have done her. She understood the power of narrative on some instinctual level. Her time in the slammer had given her the tag of 'political prisoner' and status as a permanent underdog. If it was hard to speak out against her before without looking like a bully, it was damn near impossible for any major party figure to do so from that point on.

And then Hanson got out with her conviction overturned. Any working-class or Aboriginal person in prison for unpaid parking fines or fudging their taxes would have been left to serve out their sentence for want of a good lawyer, but Hanson had enough pull to lodge an appeal that got her out of Wacol Correctional Facility on 6 November 2003.

It took just a year for her to reappear in the public eye, clinging to relevance through the magic of reality TV. She performed on *Dancing with the Stars* and *Who Wants to be a Millionaire*. She told Andrew Denton she had changed, and she was going to do better.

And she never stopped probing for that next opening, running for office in 1998, 2001, 2003, 2004, 2007, 2009, 2011, 2013 and 2015.

All she needed was another clean shot, and in 2016, two decades on, she got one.

Chapter 3

ONE NATION UNDER TRUMP

ONE NATION COULDN'T BELIEVE THAT TRUMP WAS PRESIDENT.

The votes hadn't even finished being counted that day when the One Nation crowd gathered eagerly in front of federal parliament to shoot a live Facebook video celebrating Trump's victory.

The backdrop was the front entrance to Parliament House, those doors that open wide into the marbled public halls and the winding corridors behind them. The Australian flag flew high above it, against an overcast sky that day. Pauline Hanson and Senator Malcolm Roberts stood side by side, though Senators Rodney Culleton and Brian Burston were nowhere to be seen.

'Hi everyone …' Hanson said to the camera. 'I'm so excited that Donald Trump looks like he's just over the line … And I'm so happy about it because this is putting out a clear message to everyone around the world that people power is now happening,' she gushed.

It happened with Brexit, it happened with One Nation, she said, and now it happened with Trump. Australia was next, she said, and as far as she was concerned, she was living proof.

Standing next to Malcolm Roberts was the curious figure of Tony Heller, a geologist from New Mexico in the United States. It was easy to get lost in his deep, double-barrelled American accent if you didn't know his story. Heller, as it happened, was a crackpot anti-climate-change blogger who also wrote under the pen name 'Steven Goddard'. He had never had a job related to climatology or weather systems, but he did have a blog and a Twitter feed through which he could make grand statements about things he knew only a little about. He was uncompromising and proud, shouting down his critics and comparing climate-change activists to ISIS fighters. He had flown into the country to attend what would end up being a disastrous press conference with Senator Malcolm Roberts on the 'lie' that is climate change.

'This is an incredible day for America and for Australia and our new relationship,' Heller said.

'And congratulations to the whole planet because we will free the world of this rubbish that is climate change,' Roberts added.

'It's all about people power and I'm so happy,' Pauline continued to gush, before pulling new-hire Darren Brady Nelson into frame. Nelson wore thick-rimmed glasses and a trademark thick red tie. He was holding a bottle of Black Pig and at first looked a little sheepish.

To be fair, Nelson had never sought any kind of public attention, it was the party who dragged him into the spotlight. He was a dual citizen of the United States and Australia who, Hanson said, had worked for two months as part of Donald Trump's election campaign. James Ashby, Hanson's chief of staff, had told a community meeting at Rockhampton Town Hall on 16 September 2016 that the party had hired 'one of the world's leading economists' and former economic advisor to Donald Trump.

No one had heard a word about the new hire since that moment, but here he was being rolled out for the world to see. It didn't take five minutes for reporters to start to run down his background. As it turned out, the man who had been hired to help One Nation 'build credibility on the economics front' didn't have a resume dominated by high-profile government and university appointments. Instead it was a series of short-term gigs in lower-level positions at government departments and large corporations, rounded off with involvement in a string of radical free-market think tanks.

As Philip Dorling later documented for the Australia Institute, Nelson had written about climate change for the folksy-named Heartland Institute, based in Illinois, which exists to 'discover, develop and promote free-market solutions to social and economic problems'. Nelson had previously written an essay for the Ludwig von Mises Institute, based in Auburn, Alabama, calling for the radical deregulation of the US economy, 'as much as possible, as fast as possible'. He was an 'Associated Senior Fellow' of the Center for Freedom and Prosperity, which lobbied in support of offshore tax havens. In October 2015, the dual US–Australian national had come home and got involved with LibertyWorks, an Australian free-market think tank based in Brisbane, as its 'chief economist and deputy start-up manager'.

Nelson had gone to work on the Trump campaign after a friend at the Cato Institute, a Libertarian think tank, set him up with the gig. In the entire two-month period he spent there, he had zero one-on-one time with Trump; he was only involved in the campaign as a junior member of a large team of economic analysts working out of Trump Tower and was then snatched from obscurity by One Nation.

As far as One Nation went, this was a turning point. Until then, the party had been a small but fanatical movement of Australian nationalists, each chasing their own unique vision of an Australia that no longer existed. Then, it was a protectionist party, of the 'Buy Australian' variety. Now, it was hard-wiring itself into international networks of climate-change deniers and obscure ideologically driven think tanks. In other words, One Nation was now speaking with an American accent.

As Nelson poured the champagne, Hanson's cup overflowed. After filling each glass he stopped to give a shout-out to his former economics team on the Trump campaign. Pauline then chimed in to call for unity and bipartisan support for a man who had conquered by dividing the nation.

'All I can say to people out there,' Pauline added, 'if you didn't have your support behind Donald Trump, or didn't vote for him, the whole fact is that please give the man a go. As I have always said, the more the media, the more the major political parties and everyone is against you, the more reason they are there for the people. At least give him a go for four years. And let's see what happens. But to Donald Trump. Cheers.'

It was a line that doubled as a statement about her own political fortunes and betrayed a deeply limited understanding of the world outside her own personal bubble. Donald Trump, the slick billionaire New Yorker who emphasised his talking points with wild hand gestures, infiltrated and bent the Republican Party to his will. He then marshalled its campaign machinery and drove the party all the way to the Oval Office. Hanson, the small-business owner who had stepped up to play the game from the outside ever since she was booted from the Liberal Party, had relied mostly on volunteers and diehards who were willing to suspend disbelief and sacrifice everything for the movement.

Trump, meanwhile, dominated every television channel during his campaign. Every speech, every comment, every Trump moment was beamed into American living rooms, and shared across social media for good measure. Hanson preferred to avoid journalists wherever possible, giving her time instead to early-morning talk shows where she could safely avoid pesky questions about race or her operation. Unless a reporter got in her face, it was impossible to gain access to her, and even then her aides would sometimes call the cops, which fed the narrative that Hanson was under assault by the media. By the end of 2016, Hanson stopped issuing press releases except over social media and banned the ABC from covering her events. She didn't want coverage, didn't need coverage, and she certainly didn't need transparency. Reporters' emails went unanswered, disappearing into James Ashby's inbox. Pauline wanted the votes of ordinary people, but she didn't want to put up with annoying questions about what she was doing in their name. The media were all liars anyway. Who needed them? Not Pauline, that's for damn sure. All she needed was a few thousand votes.

Something was happening out there, she could feel it, and it was big. This was global, though that wasn't the word she would use. If Trump could do it, so could she. If she could replicate what he had done, if she could bring in some of those Big American Ideas and make them work Down Under, maybe, just maybe, she would be vindicated. All the slights and tragedies and venom she had endured over the previous twenty years, the prison time and the betrayal and the insults, would be worth it.

After all, she had done it first, before Brexit, before Trump, all the way back in '96. She had championed a bizarre ethno-nationalism before the internet helped similar groups network their way across the planet, and it had made her one of the most recognisable Australians alongside Crocodile Dundee and his flesh-and-blood counterpart, Steve Irwin. No, she was no Trump, but they were cut from the same cloth. This was happening the world over. Soon, it would be her turn and then she would show them all that blind, dumb persistence worked.

So, together, the four supped champagne as they stared down the barrel of the camera. Malcolm Roberts let out a crackling whoop.

The revolution had arrived.

Chapter 4

NOWHERE TO RUN, NOWHERE TO HIDE

THE MORNING AFTER THE US ELECTION RESULT WAS KNOWN, A subdued Senator Nick Xenophon made his way downstairs from his Senate suite to the Senate entrance, as usual, where a bank of TV cameras was waiting, as usual. It was the mood that was unusual that day: sullen and depressed. It was all pervasive, across the entire building, and even the irrepressible Nick Xenophon seemed flat.

'I wonder why everyone is so down?' he asked no one in particular and no one replied.

No one could believe Trump was President, least of all the senator from South Australia, who in the weeks leading up to the vote had joked that if Trump actually won, he would have his mate Bruno, the bobcat driver, build him a bunker in his backyard so he could wait out the coming radioactive storm. Everyone, including me, thought Bruno was a character Nick had invented to get the attention of the commercial television networks, which lapped it up. Then one day I caught the screen of his smartphone as Bruno called to ask what Nick was doing blasting his name across all major news networks.

'Mate, I'm giving you free advertising,' Nick told him.

Xenophon was no Trump. He may have shared similar views on the value of manufacturing as an essential component of the economy, but everything else about the man offended everything Nick respected in a politician, and a person.

He, as it happened, had been a Bernie Sanders guy. He saw in the socialist senator from Vermont someone willing to challenge the basic assumptions of American political life, and he respected that. Sanders may have called himself a socialist, but he was calling for a fairer America in a way that would not be out of place in the right wing of the Labor Party, or even the left wing of the Libs, as far as Nick was concerned. Sanders wanted an Australian-style Medicare system, access to education and a decent minimum wage. Sanders was even speaking Nick's language when he questioned the way free-trade agreements had been negotiated and managed over the years. To a generation of Americans raised on the idea that the individual hero raged against the collective masses, that they were each temporarily embarrassed millionaires, it might have been heresy, but when Sanders pointed out that society was not a level playing field, Xenophon found himself in furious agreement.

After Bernie failed to make the cut, Hillary was the next-best option. She may not have been inspiring, she may not have been charismatic, but she certainly was better than Trump, a man Nick considered wildly irrational and painfully deceptive.

'There's no way Trump can win,' Nick once said as he walked into the office and gazed up at the television screen, which was playing a news report about the US election in the lead-up to the vote. 'No way.'

When Trump did, it seemed to change everything. Nick was a twenty-year veteran of state and federal parliaments. He had started his career as a crusading personal-injury lawyer, until he took his fight to the South Australian state parliament on a single issue and discovered an identity as a crusading politician who always went down swinging. It was poker machines that launched his career in those days, but that didn't stop him taking on other issues he felt actually mattered to ordinary people, such as ticket scalping and reliability of the electricity grid.

Then, as now, reporters would parachute in from the big east-coast cities to write about the one-man band with a degree of fascination. They wanted to watch him work, so they came to observe his quirks and habits and decide for themselves whether he was just another crazy member of the Senate crossbench, or something else entirely.

They would learn how Nick Xenophon didn't drink coffee but had a sweet tooth, and how he loathed being called Senator and asked them to call him Nick. It was a policy I assumed he had picked up to keep him grounded, in the same way political advisor Louis Howe would humble US President Franklin D. Roosevelt by refusing to use his title and only speaking to him as Franklin. In the time they would spend together, Nick would overwhelm with courtesy and care. He cracked jokes, apologised unnecessarily and got personally involved in the lives of those his office helped.

When his quirks weren't enough, reporters focussed on his origins. They learned that he was born in 1959 to parents who had met at a bus stop on Magill Road; that his father had made a business developing a block of land at Magill; that he was raised Greek Orthodox but wasn't devout and never flaunted it; and that he had been private-school educated. Then they wanted to know about his university days, and how he had been a member of the Young Liberals who had flirted with Labor but would later decide on neither.

Whatever they asked, he always had a line in reserve.

'Some kids do drugs, I was a member of the Young Liberals,' he would tell them when they asked about his time with the Liberal Party.

They would ask about that time he taught law to Christopher Pyne, and what he had been like as a student during his time at university, way back before Pyne became a minister.

'I taught him everything he doesn't know,' was all that Nick would say.

Almost always, he defied expectation. Those who loathed him the most tended to be ideological warriors and political purists who took one look at the man and instantly imagined him in the likeness of their most convenient enemy. To those on the left, he was right wing and a secret Liberal. To those on the right, he was an anti-market protectionist, a vicious slur in their world; they talked about him in the same frothy language the left reserves for racists.

What most of these people wanted was a man who was clearly left or right, but Nick Xenophon would always surprise. One analysis of his voting patterns during July 2014 and March 2016 published by *The Guardian*'s Datablog found he was in agreement with the Greens 67 per cent of the time, Labor 54 per cent and Liberal 39 per cent.

His unpredictability was amplified by his habit of holding back until he saw an opening. He never declared a position on an issue when he felt there were too many variables in play to get a sense of what the outcome would be. When someone made a misstep he never denounced them, and in doing so he always kept open the possibility of redemption. When he was attacked, he rarely hit back, instead using the display to paint himself as the underdog.

These made for effective tactics. The longer he delayed until the final moment, the greater the news interest and the more time he bought himself to work the angles. His refusal to call out others' missteps made people more willing to cooperate with him on a piece of legislation, or negotiate over an amendment. Finding himself the victim of a personal attack reinforced the idea among his supporters that he was doing something right.

Few, however, could recognise the programming at the heart of Nick Xenophon's political machine. During an interview, someone would bring up the usual clichés about his centrist politics and then Nick would often ask whether the reporter had heard of Ted Halstead, co-author of *The Future of American Politics: The Radical Center.* None had, and to my knowledge, none ever bothered to check Halstead out. Noel Pearson was the Australian who coined the term 'radical centre', and no one had time to sit down with an American political treatise. Halstead's work described a politics that was radical in its willingness to reform institutions for the better, and centrist in its rejection of ideology as a driving force, in favour of a pragmatic, inclusive politics.

It was a politics that confused and angered political die-hards for reasons Ted Halstead's co-author, Michael Lind, described for *Salon* magazine in 2010. Radical centrist politics, he said, rejects both the neoliberalism of the hard right as beneficial only to the rich, and the identity politics of the left, 'in favor of an optimistic, inclusive vision of an American melting pot that blends races as well as white ethnic groups'.

Nick Xenophon's innovation was his keen sense of marketing and an early recognition that politics was rapidly reshaping around the question of how to manage the process of globalisation. Adelaide was his city and it lay at the end of a major river system, with a dying manufacturing base and rising unemployment. Every day, its best sons and daughters were boarding planes to Melbourne. His politics attempted to walk the line between left and right, moving nimbly between the issues to get the best result.

So to the public he spoke plainly, he was hardworking and he made a point of being seen to be hardworking. At his best, there were almost daily press conferences, and he led the news on every channel, even as reporters on the political beat whispered about getting yet another call to another goddamn Nick Xenophon presser.

But then, he understood something about politics most did not: if a politician writes a letter to a minister on an issue, and no one hears about it on the evening news, did it make a sound?

With this, he took up causes big and small. For subcontractors in the building industry, he wanted to set up a regime to ensure they got paid, even after a company that contracted them had collapsed. For young people he had waged a decade-long fight over ticket scalping, writing to Adele's management for a meeting with the singer. For general aviation pilots, he dressed down the CEO of Qantas in a speech given to an aviation industry dinner where he was in attendance. In 2009 he started a public fight with Scientology when no one else would, calling them a cult and denouncing their cruelty. For an ice addict whose life was slowly crumbling under the weight of her addiction, he was willing to fight what seemed to most of his electorate office staff to be a lost cause.

'My job is to help get people through the door so that they have a chance,' he once scolded me. 'We help people. That's what we do.'

And if anyone ever doubted the courage of his convictions, he could always point to how he had been tear-gassed in Kuala Lumpur and banned from Malaysia over his support for his friend, dissident Malaysian politician Anwar Ibrahim. Or how in 2009 he was willing to hold up former Prime Minister Kevin Rudd's $1 billion stimulus package until Rudd allocated more funding to help the Murray River. Or how he had released his entire personal tax return to Laurie Oakes and had offered it to other reporters to demonstrate his commitment to transparency.

All of which played well to every voter who had watched a politician make big promises to get elected and do a lot of nothing about it once in office.

* * *

Nick worked at a breathless pace. It was his brand, but also his personal habit, driven in part by an acute sense of his own mortality. Sometimes, it expressed itself as hypochondria, and sometimes it was a genuine life-threatening issue, like the time in 2002 he underwent open heart surgery and was forced to confront the possibility he might never get up from the table. He had always had a nervous sense of his own mortality, but when he woke up, that awareness deepened. Something about it tapped into a dark, depressive streak in his character that coloured his sense of humour. Life could be funny and humour took the edge off, but living was no joke. The clock was always ticking and its hands spoke like thunder.

So, he threw himself into his work like the world was about to end. He said yes to everything and worked from seven in the morning till ten at night, on an average day. Anything involving Canberra in his diary was coloured red, and in sitting weeks there were no gaps, just an endless streak of fire-truck red. Some days he operated on three or four hours' sleep, and by the end of a sitting period, it started to show on both Nick and his staff. Tensions were high, nerves were frayed and tempers could be short. The only thing that kept it all together was the solidarity of the trench.

It also helped that he was a consummate performer, charismatic and personable. No matter what time of day, or how broken he felt by the intense schedule he kept, when it came time to do the interview or give the speech, he would switch on, drawing a reserve of energy from somewhere deep within himself.

Playing the game from outside the major parties had been freeing for Nick Xenophon. Much of a politician's vitality is spent scheming a way to a position of power and influence. When they get there, they have too much to lose to do much of anything. Staying independent and then founding his own minor party meant Nick could focus instead on being a colossal pain in the arse to anyone he thought a bully. Among the crossbench, this quality, along with his experience and innate sense of solidarity, meant every time a new personality found their way into federal parliament, they found their way to him. He had been around so long, he had seen every tactic and trick, and operated with a firm grasp of what was needed to survive in a place that could be insular and venomous.

And he was happy to share. All he asked in return was cooperation.

* * *

Trump, though he may have been a world away, seemed to up-end everything Nick knew about electoral politics. He was struggling to process the change that had taken place that first week when senior Fairfax political reporter Peter Hartcher pinned him down for a quiet interview late one evening in the staff cafeteria.

Hartcher is a legend, though I did not know his mythology when I sat down next to him. He is a precise, neatly groomed, soft-spoken man who keeps a tiny notebook in the breast pocket of his suit jacket in which he writes tiny, exact script. That week he was talking about the same thing everyone else was: Trump.

Trump was the man who had ridden a wave of discontent into office, but wasn't Nick Xenophon doing the same with his baby political party, the Nick Xenophon Team? The party had secured three Senate seats and a seat in the House of Representatives at the last federal election, in a state that at times felt like the rest of Australia was abandoning it.

So, Hartcher wanted to know, what did Nick Xenophon truly think of Donald Trump?

'You know, his slogan, "Drain the Swamp", I think there's probably a good line in that,' Nick Xenophon said. 'Trump says he is trying to drain the swamp, but he's going to swim in it. He's going to be doing backstroke through it.'

He stopped himself.

'That doesn't quite work, I need to play with that a bit more.'

What he was trying to say was that while Donald Trump may have campaigned on a promise to drain the swamp, in the end, he was going to bathe in it. Trump's network of corporate and business connections, and his complete disregard for truth, meant that it wouldn't take long before influence peddlers and cronyism set in.

But then, Donald Trump's essential character wasn't what caused Nick so much trouble in the immediate aftermath of Election Day. True to form, the first thing he had done once he knew the outcome was to put out a press release calling for the US–Australian alliance to be revisited on the basis that Donald Trump was so reckless, it was a real possibility that he could end up dragging Australia into a catastrophic war, though the concept of a nuclear holocaust wasn't what gripped him most. Instead it was the very notion of a 'post-truth politics' that grabbed at the heart of Nick Xenophon. In all his personal dealings, he placed a premium on truth and verifiable fact. Losing his trust lost it forever. This was a quality he projected out onto the world and it meant his office was expert in the art of the Freedom of Information request. Any rat who wound up being cross-examined by Senator Nick Xenophon during a Senate Estimates committee hearing would take their seat at the bench knowing it was just a matter of time before he would draw his claws and pounce.

For him, to watch a politician lie so openly and shamelessly through an election campaign was truly alarming. If a candidate in a stable liberal-democracy could say anything and still take power, where was the limit? How do you campaign against someone like that? Any voter listening to a Trump campaign speech would simply hear what they wanted to hear and dismiss the rest as campaign rhetoric. And how could someone like that possibly be restrained by embarrassment or shame once in power? The potential damage that person could do was immeasurable.

What if it happened here?

These were tactics Nick had experienced to some extent during the 2016 federal election, he told Hartcher, when Labor effectively inoculated its base against the appeal of voting for the NXT (Nick Xenophon Team) by claiming its leader wanted to abolish penalty rates and had voted to privatise ETSA (Electricity Trust of South Australia) in the '90s. Both claims were false, and despite the damage, out of that election Senators Stirling Griff and Skye Kakoschke-Moore were elected to the Senate, and Rebekha Sharkie made it into the Lower House.

'I think everything is changing,' Nick said, towards the end of their conversation. 'We saw the first-term Campbell Newman government thrown out in Queensland with something like a 20 per cent swing. I don't know what is going to happen. It's all or nothing. I think no one is safe right now. Everyone's seat is up for grabs, including mine.'

Chapter 5
THE POLITICS OF POLITICS

POLITICS IS A PROFESSION IN WHICH FAILURE IS INEVITABLE.
Every day politicians face up to the reality that the very issues that drove them to politics in the first place are unlikely to be resolved, and they have a better chance of fading into a distant memory than achieving name recognition, let alone anything truly significant with their time in office.

The daily grind of a politician mostly involves navigating the tit-for-tat point-scoring in the games played out between major parties, corporate entities, the media, government departments and bureaucracies, and holding meetings, following procedure and trying not to make the wrong people mad. As a profession, politicians are expected to have a considered opinion on every issue of public life, despite how impossible that task is, and then they're expected to sit quietly while having that opinion ruthlessly dissected by everyone else. For a politician, it is always better to appear ignorant than have no opinion at all.

Their work environment is Parliament House. Fawning documentary makers and tour guides may hail the building as an architectural triumph, but in function it serves as a citadel of Australian democracy. As a building, its internal layout is a rabbit's warren of corridors and chambers and suites and meeting rooms atop a subterranean network of catacombs and supply corridors that allow those who clean the urinals and serve the food to go about without having to spend too much time in the halls of power.

Move through this environment long enough and it is easy to understand how an elected representative of the people might go through their day without ever engaging with the outside world in any meaningful way.

If they don't live in Canberra, they will fly into the city on a Sunday night ahead of a sitting week. If they are so inclined, they may have access to their airline's executive lounge, where they are served a restaurant-quality meal for free before boarding. There, they will find themselves in the company of other elected representatives and CEOs.

If they are loose with the public purse, they can board their flight and fly business class. They'll tell their critics that it helps them work. When they land, they will take a taxi from the airport to wherever it is they stay. In the morning, they will wake to be driven to Parliament House in a Commonwealth car. They might talk to the driver, often a former lower-level public servant who knows the value of discretion and deference to authority. Or they might not.

Inside each parliamentary suite there is a private kitchen, a private office, and a private bathroom, complete with showers and a second door that opens into the hall, which allows them to quietly slip away without the three o'clock appointment in their waiting area knowing they were ever in. Most will open the office to their staff, but they don't have to. Most won't use the second door, but they can.

At lunchtime, the scale and design of the building makes leaving a chore. This means there is no cafe down the road and no bakery to visit. There is the coffee cart, maybe, but coffee and copy is the job of a junior staffer. There is the staff cafeteria, known as The Trough, or Aussies Cafe, but these are another public arena in political life and should be trod with care.

Their week is filled with committee hearings, with inquiries, with the slow grind of Estimates Hearings, meetings with lobbyists or representatives of organisations, phone calls to constituents, power breakfasts or cocktail parties. Or they can instruct their staff to clear the diary entirely.

And at the end, when it's over, they head back to the airport lounge to await another business-class flight home, unless they make a point of flying cattle class.

This is an environment that breeds isolation and loneliness. A workaholic is no different from an alcoholic and might never leave. In doing so, they forget who it is they work for. Disconnected from their roots, removed from social movements, an idealist might find their passion dulled. Those with families miss out on being a part of the defining moments of their children's lives. Some may come to resent the criticism that comes with the job, and so end up feeling a little too entitled to the perks their station affords.

For a candidate chosen by 100 000 people and sent off to the nation's capital, it doesn't take long before the ease and familiarity of the place take over. If it weren't for the election cycle, it would be easy to wind out the years in Canberra's loving embrace, a company town where politics and government are the only industry worth being in, where everyone is a free agent, and where the only thing that matters is the integrity of the brand.

At the heart of it all is Parliament House, which is high school with six-figure salaries and the added thrill of palace intrigue. It's about who is talking to whom or, rather, who is seen talking to whom. It's who has the best relationship with the other side; it's those who have to walk across the room to start a conversation, and those who only need to wait for the world to come to them. It's where you live, how high your security clearance, your pedigree, what schools you went to and who can vouch for you.

Those at the top of the pyramid in this world are the Permanent Class, the narrow group of elected representatives, advisors, academics, lobbyists, journalists and bureaucrats who live and work in Canberra. Cabinet members and ministers are included by virtue of their position, even if they are Fly-In-Fly-Out (FIFO). These are the people whose whole lives revolve around parliament in one way or another.

When not in parliament they have power breakfasts at the same restaurants, drink at the same bars, and go to the same cocktail parties. They know how the country is run, and what matters, because they are the ones who decide how the country is run and what matters.

After that there is the FIFO Class, those advisors and electorate office staffers who fly into parliament on a Sunday night for a sitting week, and then leave again that Thursday. They are the hopefuls, the climbers and the people with mortgages to pay. They are the ones who keep the machinery of parliament turning. They draft the letters, give advice, answer the phones, run the meetings, organise the press conferences and take the notes. They are only supposed to work forty-hour weeks, but they go home when they are done, and their work is rarely done, unless their office is one with a reputation for being quiet. They are insiders by proximity, and trusted by necessity.

At the bottom of the pyramid is everyone else. These are the people who don't work in politics, also referred to as the 'constituents', 'the electorate', 'the public' and 'the voters', pretty much anyone who gets talked about in official media releases and press conferences with absolute certainty, but who rarely speaks for themselves. They are complete outsiders, they are the letter writers, the protesters, the people who sign petitions, the people with issues to be solved or evaded, the apathetic and the hostile.

These people live somewhere else, somewhere 'out there'.

To those within the world of politics, these people are also largely abstract. In the mind of a politician, the voters are a vast mass of people all clumped together with a narrow set of wants and needs. Individually, they only become 'real' when they turn up for meetings, or are heard as a voice on the other end of a telephone call made to an electorate office, a phone call that will rarely make its way to the ear of an elected representative. This is called 'access', and few people outside of politics have it. Those who do have what is called a 'relationship'.

Another way they can become 'real' is when they become inconvenient, which makes them a risk to be managed. A protest group might interrupt an elected representative's daily routine by turning up where they should not. This is called a 'security risk'. When it is insignificant, it is called 'silly' or 'immature'. When it is significant, it is described as 'inappropriate' or 'highly inappropriate'.

Alternatively, a person might stop an elected representative during a carefully stage-managed public appearance to ask them direct questions, or someone might appear in the audience of a televised political forum and ask a question from their own lived experience. How the elected representative responds is the candidate's 'performance'. How it looks to the outside world is called 'optics'. Optics are bad when a representative or government bureaucrat comes out looking stupid, ill-informed or downright cruel. They are good when everyone watching knows that their man or woman is the hero, and the others villains.

An extension of this is the 'sales job'. The job description of the prime minister and senior ministers is the same as vacuum-cleaner salespeople: know the product, show off its features, answer the questions and move it to the register. Sure, some people aren't going to like what's on offer, or their very presence, but then, pragmatic politics is all about 'net positives' and 'net negatives'. So long as the number of voters that are picked up with a policy outweigh those that are lost, everything is golden.

It's why a government should never make the mistake of listening too much to opposition. Protesters might march and columnists might type, but in the end it's the government that has the 'mandate' to be there. All questions about what is to be done were supposed to have been decided and locked in at the last election. Any discontent among those outside of politics is just the product of an ignorant public.

'If they only understood,' the conversation goes, before concluding that no reasonable person would disagree. People, of course, are entitled to their opinions, but mostly these opinions are reactions to what has already been decided by the Permanent Class. This is called the 'agenda', and what everyone else out there doesn't understand is that today's debate is the product of yesterday's decision-making.

The public are the audience. Their role is to quietly marvel as the great drama unfolds, to laugh and clap at every twist, and hiss the rise, or fall, of another character on the national stage.

This is called 'the process'. This is Pauline Hanson's enemy.

Chapter 6

A STUDY IN PERSPECTIVE

THE SECOND-WORST JOB IN POLITICS IS THAT OF MEDIA advisor.

In politics, the media advisor is a spokesperson, a diplomat, a marketing advisor, a confidant, a personal driver, a speechwriter and an intern. Their job is to handle all communications with the outside world, to maintain the integrity of the brand, to be across every issue the candidate is across, to frame the image, keep an eye on what's happening in the background and to play defence when reporters play offence.

Most of all, their job is to make sure people can always tell the hero from the villain. Politics is a game of images and perceptions played out on people's television sets, a whirring twenty-four-hour beast with a powerful hunger for visuals and commentary, a non-stop, never-ending appetite for novelty and a fish-bowl memory. Every event is dissected for what it means. A panel of experts can spend six hours pulling apart a political speech, examining each word for clues to its true intent, when time pressures meant it had taken just twenty minutes to dash off the text. Two commentators may bicker and yell for an hour and never really say anything. The media does not care whether you are having a bad day. The media hungers for content and the machine must be fed.

To operate in this environment, a media advisor must learn the politics of the Canberra Press Gallery, the closed shop that houses the cream of the nation's associated press. They are the old lions and young guns who have climbed the ladder to be closer to the action and get themselves invited to the same political functions and cocktail parties as the people they cover. There they develop relationships and so write the tacit contract that exists between the Parliament House press corps and their subjects that ensures them access.

And just like their subjects, the Press Gallery has its own internal politics. It's print publications versus digital media, free commercial TV networks versus the ABC versus *Sky News*. Don't tell *Today* you're booking them the same weekend as *Sunrise*. Don't go on the ABC without doing the commercials. Be careful talking to that Fairfax editor, he's got a nasty reputation. That guy from *The Australian* couldn't report the weather straight. Is the boss too busy to talk to that reporter? Well, the next headline will cut them to pieces.

A smart media advisor plays this game well. They know which reporters' calls should be returned immediately, and whose can be triaged. They know which commentators hate the boss, and which are friendly. They know how to deflect attention when things go bad, and what line to run that gets the message across but also defuses the tension.

When it goes right, it can be magic. When the Australian BBHO syndicate challenged Gina Rinehart for control of the Kidman Cattle Empire, the whole story had the feel of an old-school western. Rinehart was the black hat, the mining oligarch backed by Chinese money intent on taking over one of Australia's biggest agricultural businesses. The white hats were the four cowboys from wealthy agricultural families whose initials gave the syndicate its name, led by Sterling Buntine, a man built like a mountain who had secured finance to help the group go toe-to-toe with Rinehart.

To get the word out, Buntine had sought help from Nick Xenophon and Bob Katter. The all-Australian bid neatly fitted with Nick Xenophon's Buy Australian push and squared easily with Bob Katter's defence of the country's farmers. They were also both veteran political operators who knew how to make a lot of noise.

Together they had called a joint press conference and made a few personal phone calls to critical editors, and when it came time to roll out, Xenophon, Buntine and Katter had left Katter's office on the House of Reps side of parliament where a News Corp photographer had been shooting their photo. Together, they walked out to meet the press, who were waiting in Mural Hall, level two.

Nick had always disliked the entourage look, and never let his staff escort him on the way to a presser. Katter's chief of staff was the only one present from his office at that moment and she went ahead to see if anyone was there. The moment she turned the corner, she doubled back. Her eyes were wide with fear and awe.

'There are more cameras than I have ever seen,' she said.

Every camera in the building seemed to have been switched on for the showdown between the two giants, and as Buntine took his place behind the branded microphones, his hands holding his prepared statement shook. For a civilian, staring down the barrel of one camera is hard enough, let alone a bank of them arranged like a firing squad. Some people have trouble speaking to an audience of ten, but right then, in that moment, Buntine was about to address a nation of twenty-four million people with a message that would be heard as far away as China. For the next twenty-four hours, he led the news in every paper, on every channel and across social media.

Buntine ultimately lost, outgunned by Gina Rinehart's access to what seemed like a limitless pool of Chinese money. In media terms, it was a win for the little guys, a made-for-TV moment that gave the political leaders of two separate minor parties a chance to outflank the majors and steal their oxygen by going all-in for a group who, in their own way, were challenging business as usual.

It was also unusual in a sense. Once upon a time, Buntine would have gone to the majors for such a thing, but this time he didn't ask the Nationals, or even the Liberals, for help. Gina Rinehart had close friends in those circles, such as Barnaby Joyce, to whose campaign she had donated $50 000. Instead, Buntine had gone to the minor parties and leveraged their relationship with the media to get the word out.

It was a model for how independents and minor parties worked the media, and the media worked them. But then, the machine operated without fear or favour. When news broke of a feud between Rodney Culleton, the bumbling

One Nation senator who found himself in the media for all the wrong reasons, and his party leader, the media swarmed.

'I feel sorry for them,' one NXT advisor from another office said after coming back from a visit to Culleton's suite. It was the day Culleton had been referred to the High Court with a majority that included his own party leader, and they had gone over to discuss an upcoming vote. 'They're in crisis. Everyone's running around. No one has any idea. It's chaos.'

And it was just the start. One Nation bucked the trend among minor parties and independents who desperately try to cultivate a good relationship with local and national media. In Pauline's world, transparency was a stick with which to beat government institutions and bureaucrats, but an unnecessary virtue when it came to One Nation.

Hanson has always treated the media with a degree of cynicism. They are traitorous, and never report the truth – or, rather, her truth. Hanson might have once invited Margo Kingston to stay in her home overnight and even let the *Sydney Morning Herald* reporter wear her clothes, but by the end of her 1998 campaign for re-election, her advisor David Oldfield was inciting mobs to attack journalists covering her campaign and cancelling events at the last minute, forcing them to chase her through the streets of rural towns at speed.

Nothing had really changed when Hanson returned to federal parliament in 2016, despite the Liberal Party's Arthur Sinodinos telling a press conference that she was more 'sophisticated' this time around, an appraisal with which Nick Xenophon agreed. Politically, he was no friend of Hanson, but his assessment was that she had mellowed with age and wasn't as quick to come across the table with a knife between her teeth, making her better able to use her influence to achieve good outcomes. As proof he pointed to Hanson's intervention in the dispute between Wilmar, a Singaporean-owned agribusiness company that runs eight sugar mills and produces over half the sugar in Australia, and the Queensland sugar-cane farmers in rebellion because they felt squashed by one of the most powerful commodity traders in the world.

Whether or not that was true, her relationship with the media, and her attitude to transparency, were still hostile.

The first blow was struck when Malcolm Roberts called a press conference to talk about climate change, but James Ashby shut the whole thing down when reporters refused to follow One Nation's script. A similar situation occurred when Rodney Culleton wanted to appear on *Paul Murray Live* and Ashby, wisely, tried to stop him from doing it out of fear for what the party's loose cannon would say. Culleton, defiant to a fault, did the interview anyway, and it made for painful viewing.

To get to Hanson, reporters had to go through James Ashby. Hanson was his product, and she was in demand, so he tightly controlled access. Anyone he wanted to impress could meet Hanson. Anyone who couldn't benefit him in some way was shut out.

'Thanks but no thanks,' was all he said to one reporter who emailed looking for an interview. They were lucky: to others he didn't respond at all, forcing them to seek out other One Nation staffers as a form of back-channel diplomacy.

There was a sense that James Ashby still burned with anger at the way he had been treated throughout the Peter Slipper scandal. He had no friends in the media, he once told a One Nation staffer, though this was something all veteran political operators felt on some level. Still, Ashby's general approach seemed to be that either a reporter earned his trust, or they would be shut out. Reporters were dogs to be brought to heel and fed, or put down. That was it.

Under his watch, the party would stop issuing press releases and only distribute information over social media. Donald Trump didn't need the media, so why did Pauline Hanson? They had Twitter and Facebook to speak directly to their supporters through videos uploaded from whichever country back road Hanson happened to be travelling. Trump might have had 21.8 million Twitter followers compared to Hanson's 26 000, but that was mere detail. Just like Trump, Hanson is notorious, and that's all she needs to get a run on the evening news.

In part, this is motivated by a growing frustration with leaks to the press.

Leaks generally happen in one of two ways.

The first is to punish a rival. In mid-February 2017, Nick Xenophon along with Skye Kakoschke-Moore and Rebekha Sharkie met with Scott Morrison for negotiations over the government's proposed childcare package. During the meeting, the NXT senators told him they would block the government's legislation. In front of the others, Morrison asked for a private chat with Xenophon, man to man. Nick declined. Anything the minister had to say could be said in front of his colleagues, Nick said. The next day a story appeared in the *Daily Telegraph* claiming that Nick Xenophon had 'lost control of his own party', and an unnamed minister told the paper that negotiating with the South Australian senator was 'like wrestling with smoke'.

When I asked Nick about it, all he would say was that other politicians had quietly told him how awful the story was.

'They were horrified because it would increase my vote in South Australia,' he said.

Those leaks that don't come direct to the media tend to happen in a three-step process. A staffer has had a long day and goes for a drink with a friend. Over a beer they tell that friend about what happened in that crazy meeting they were in. People love gossip and because having the inside scoop makes them feel special, that friend tells the next three people they meet, one of whom happens to be a reporter. A couple of days later, the staffer opens up their morning paper or clicks onto an article about their office.

Huh, they think. *I wonder where they got that from.*

If you're One Nation, leaks happen because you burn people. James Ashby called them 'squeaky wheels' in the press, but they were often ex-staffers who had been purged in another internal power struggle, or even currently serving staff who were increasingly alarmed. They were Hanson's disposable people, used up and replaced when they became inconvenient. If they didn't talk to a reporter directly, they would confide in a friend about the problems they had been having and that information would find its way to a journalist. The more this happened, the more Ashby cracked down on the flow of information, and the more valuable each leak became, making each story bigger than the last.

Eventually the 'relationship' boiled over into outright hostility when on the night voters went to the polls in the Western Australian state election, the ABC was banned from the One Nation election night party, despite other reporters turning up without prior approval. James Ashby told ABC staff it was a 'private function', just as David Oldfield had told the reporters he evicted from One Nation events during his tour of duty in the '90s.

Then, on 10 April 2017, two decades after One Nation first launched, Hanson announced through a video on her Facebook account that the ABC had been blacklisted. The ABC had run a story on its *Four Corners* program detailing political donations from Victorian property developer Bill McNee to One Nation that had been used to buy a light plane, and One Nation had been scrambling to find a way to cover it. Hanson's redirect was to focus her fury on the ABC's Andrew Probyn, who had been leaked information – presumably by other pols who did not want to travel with her – that Hanson was heading to Afghanistan with the Australian Defence Force to meet currently serving soldiers, which he then repeated on *Insiders*.

A reporter had received information, and Pauline Hanson expected him not to publish. It was the last straw, she said. She would no longer provide comment on stories, and the ABC would be banned from all One Nation events. Hanson and Ashby didn't care that the ABC had the biggest reach into regional Queensland, where much of her base lived. Instead they preferred the soft embrace of Channel Seven's *Sunrise*, *Sky News*'s Paul Murray and *Herald Sun* columnist Andrew Bolt. In retribution, they would demand $600 million in funding cuts to bring the ABC to heel.

Just like Donald J. Trump, who once in office railed against fake news and substituted in his own 'alternative facts', Pauline Hanson didn't need the media. She was the one everyone was talking about. She was the product. She was notorious on the left and a firebrand who stoked passions on the right. As far as she was concerned, the media needed her, and as long as that was the case, her facts were the real facts. Everything else was fiction and anyone who said otherwise was an enemy.

Chapter 7

GHOSTS IN THE MACHINE

IT WAS MID-OCTOBER WHEN THE EMAIL LANDED IN MY INBOX with an attached copy of a press release issued by Pauline Hanson, Senator for Queensland, telling the world that Nick Xenophon had 'gone soft on dole bludgers'.

Have you seen this? the email read.

I hadn't.

I hit print, and while I waited for the machine to spit it out, I read the thing.

Hanson was attacking the boss for scuttling a government plan to force young people to wait a month before they could get the dole, even though it wasn't his portfolio. Welfare had fallen to Rebekha Sharkie, and her office had been leading the charge on the issue, not Nick's. Since it was her responsibility, he preferred to let her take the lead.

'Nick doesn't get it,' the statement read. 'He's always been a lawyer, but across Australia you have young people finishing school and going straight onto the dole. Most of these kids have never worked, still live with their parents, have never paid taxes and think that for some reason this entitles them to handouts.'

As a communiqué, this was textbook Hanson. The implication was that Nick Xenophon was a wealthy professional: an elite. Soft. Effete. Unmanly. Most of all, the release suggested that Nick Xenophon was out of touch.

It was hilarious as much as it was monstrous. I couldn't help but laugh even as I read the text and thought about those people I grew up with who had been on welfare or still were. Hanson didn't know what was best for them, and in the time I spent on The Hill, I had come to learn that welfare, in a parliament where two-thirds of the members owned investment properties, gave the measure of a politician. It was the mark of a deeply cynical politician to go after people existing on below-poverty-level income with limited capacity to organise or represent their interests in federal parliament. Doing so let those politicians project an aura of strength by sending the message that the best way to help people on the bottom was to kick them while they were down. As a political gesture it was on par with 'dead child laws', those bills that propose giving greater powers to law enforcement in the aftermath of an atrocious killing of a child, and which are tagged with that child's name so no sane politician would dare vote against it. It was a tactic that was sometimes justified when the reform was necessary, but had been labelled 'low priority' and so wasn't getting the numbers. When used as a shameless act of political point scoring, it was low.

During my time in his office, Nick largely treated welfare issues with neglect. When Centrelink started trying to claim back money from people on welfare in 2016 using an automated debt-recovery system, he spoke out against the system, though he was hardly the loudest voice. After I left, in early July 2017, he was talking about bringing in a bill ahead of the South Australian election that would dock welfare payments for anyone on Centrelink caught shoplifting. He thought it would help small-business owners by cutting down the rate at which people steal, he said. In practice, it would effectively punish people who were struggling to the point of being forced to steal by slapping them with a criminal conviction and lowering their already meagre income.

When the printer spat out Hanson's statement, I handed it to Nick. He was sitting at the table in his office looking shell shocked. It was a Wednesday, in the middle of Senate Estimates, towards the end of a long year and he was running several lines of inquiry on several different issues with very little sleep. Now he had to deal with an attack coming from his right flank.

I suggested leaving it alone. All Hanson was trying to do was get some free press out of him. Television was a medium both embraced, but of the two, he did it better.

'No,' Nick said darkly, 'we need to respond to this.'

Hanson had sensed weakness and taken a shot, so the NXT fired back by calling a presser in Mural Hall, and on the way over to the cameras word came that Pauline Hanson was on Norfolk Island for a fact-finding tour during the middle of Senate Estimates. Essentially, this meant she was picking a fight while standing on a beach somewhere instead of sitting in a dark committee room performing one of a senator's most valuable tasks. It was something Hanson would make a habit of. For the first year in the job, she spent more time laying the groundwork for the next Queensland state election than she did actually performing her duties as a senator. It was only when the media shamed her in May 2017, pointing out that she had missed Estimates for the third time, that she actually made an appearance.

Nick opened the press conference by talking about how they had been working hard during Estimates, before letting Rebekha Sharkie go on to explain how she considered the one-month wait for the dole unfair. Starving young people into a job wasn't going to help lower the youth unemployment rate, she said.

Then the microphone was passed back to Nick to close it out. He was aware Pauline Hanson had a few things to say about his party's decision to judge a policy on its merits, he told the cameras, but he had also been told Senator Hanson was on Norfolk Island that week.

'And, you know, if Senator Hanson has a problem with me, or NXT's handling of issues, she is welcome to come talk to me in person.'

* * *

There are three rules to operating as an independent or minor party in the Australian parliament. The first is, be nice to your colleagues. The second is, work together where possible. The third is, always save your ammunition for the majors.

Nowhere will you find this in writing. Nowhere will you find it formally agreed upon or spoken about in public. Bob Katter has come the closest of anyone to codifying these principles.

Instead, it's more a tacit agreement based on instinct, or maybe a shared sense of self-preservation. Holding to these principles makes the independents and minor parties powerful. When they come together like flocking birds, or schooling fish, the strays form the fourth-largest political force in parliament as an emergent, decentralised political party. This is how they maximise their gains, represent their communities and ensure the Senate functions as a house of review. This is the long view, and at their best, the independents and minor parties hold to it.

When they abandon these rules and find themselves at cross purposes, the independents and minor parties are at their weakest. That's when the short view rules and a transactional approach of politics takes hold. All that matters then is maximising the return on a particular issue. Anyone who watched the debate over the backpacker tax unfold over eighteen months saw it in action. As an issue it was a dull technicality to most of the country, but to those Australians from regional or country areas who depended on backpackers to bring in their harvest, it was life or death.

What everyone could agree on, however, was that they were sick of hearing about it and just wanted it sorted out. As 2016 drew to a close, the independents worked out they had an advantage over a government that was desperate to pass legislation, and so started to look for deals. Just when one rate seemed to be set, another independent broke ranks to try to force it lower while extracting deeper concessions from the government. In the end, most would lose out, as the Greens saw advantage in the situation and with their bloc of votes gave the Liberal government their support in return for a $100 million Landcare package, effectively wiping out any money the government would have collected as a result of the tax.

As a party, One Nation defaults to the short view. Anyone who isn't an immediate political threat finds themselves co-opted into One Nation's narrative. Through her Facebook page, Hanson started to run her own gonzo chat show where she invited other senators to go through the issues and talk about the week as it was. Senators David Leyonhjelm and Jacqui Lambie would stand awkwardly around a table with Hanson in a Senate courtyard while they discussed that week's events. Both were lone senators who provided no real long-term threat to One Nation and, on some issues, could even be considered partners. Getting them to stand long enough to cooperate helped Hanson project the image that she was credible, respected and actively engaged in the work of the Senate.

Anyone who rivalled One Nation for influence could expect to be ambushed. While One Nation was happy to let Nick Xenophon and the NXT do the leg work on a series of major votes, and James Ashby once praised 'Nick Xenophon and his team' for rising above the fray, Hanson never forgets who the competition are. And in the upcoming Queensland state election that was Bob Katter.

Bob Katter, from what I could tell, was a man who greatly enjoyed being Bob Katter. He prized the role of rebel and had carefully constructed a public persona as Crazy Bob Katter, the man in the Ten Gallon Hat. He used it at times to stir the pot for fun, and he disregarded it at will, when he sensed that whomever he was speaking to underestimated him.

For the most part, Katter had always taken the long view, keeping his eyes fixed on the goal of winning the balance of power in Queensland state politics. To do it, he needed another minor party and he was looking to One Nation to fill the role.

For a while, his own people had suspected One Nation of pulling a copy-and-paste job on the Katter Australia Party's (KAP) policies, but they kept it quiet with an eye to the big picture. Then, in April 2017, the papers were reporting that the leader of One Nation's Queensland branch, Steve Dickson, a defector from the Nationals, had savaged Katter in the press. Dickson claimed the KAP had lifted One Nation's crocodile policy. It was a silly claim and a small issue in the scheme of things, but to those inside the KAP, it was an ambush that spoke more to the reliability of One Nation as partners, and caused many to reconsider a few basic assumptions about how the future would look. The two parties had signed a preference deal earlier in the year, but that apparently hadn't changed One Nation's willingness to turn on them in the press. Katter, himself, never really considered One Nation a political threat, but with that even he was starting to question their capacity for partnership.

'I don't mean to be arrogant or egotistical, I just haven't had a sense of fear with respect to Pauline,' he breathed down the phone to me one night after getting off a flight to Townsville.

'But where I have started to get toey, is that we needed her to win seats for us to have the balance of power, but looking at the voting record, she won't be voting with us.

'I started thinking we'd have the balance of power, and we can have the balance of power, but her direction is the Liberals' direction. I hear, though, that she has a good relationship with Malcolm Turnbull.'

That was a clever line by Katter. In the same way that Labor people were always quick to point out that Hanson was not working class, Katter had not only fed me the same attack line being used by all the independents who felt under pressure from Hanson, but also connected her to Malcolm Turnbull. He was talking to those parts of regional Australia where Turnbull's name translated as 'closet leftie'.

It also happened to be true. From August to December 2016, Hanson had sided with the government on 72 per cent of votes according to an analysis by lobby group Hawker Britton, and James Ashby, the man who controlled all access to Hanson, was in regular, direct contact with the Prime Minister's senior staff.

If Turnbull needed something done in the Senate, Ashby would be one of the first to know.

'Our fascination was such that she could have been from another planet, but it was also an uncomfortable reminder of the class divide. When was the last time a semi-inarticulate, "ordinary" person had blundered onto the stage where power is played out, and stayed there? ... She was the unthinkable setting her sights on the impossible.'

Margo Kingston, *Off the Rails:*
The Pauline Hanson Trip, 1999

Chapter 8

ULTRA VIRES

'ASHBY IS AN AGGRESSIVE, NASTY INDIVIDUAL,' MARGARET
Menzel remembers when talking about her stint in politics.
Her official title in those days was chief of staff to Senator
Rodney Culleton of Western Australia and the trouble
started almost from day one.

Before Margaret had signed on with Rodney, James Ashby
had made clear to Culleton in a private meeting with Pauline
Hanson in her office that he didn't want Margaret around.
Maybe it had something to do with how close Margaret
and her husband, Max, were to Bob Katter, a Hanson rival
whose party had absorbed many of those left behind when
One Nation imploded the first time. Maybe Ashby thought
she was just incompetent, or maybe Margaret didn't fit
the image of his revamped party. What was going through
Ashby's mind at any given time was unknowable, and he
seemed to like it that way.

Margaret Menzel and Rodney Culleton went back too far to let Ashby get his way. They had met as activists – though that's not the word they'd use for the work they were doing – organising farmers who wanted to push back against those looking to take their land. Four-fifths of Queensland had been in drought at the time and agricultural communities across the state were facing a debt crisis. Either the banks were looking to foreclose on the farm, the thing that defined every aspect of life for those who worked one, or coal seam gas companies were looking to explore on their land, with the potential to poison their water and render it unviable. Out of this came movements like Lock the Gate and the farmers gathering at Winton.

Something similar was happening to agricultural communities in Western Australia, though there were different underlying causes. This is why Rodney Culleton talked about going after the banks like a Bolshevik and why Margaret and her husband had worked hard on his campaign at the 2016 election and why, when it all was over, Rodney was determined to give Margaret the job in his office as chief of staff.

Margaret, though, initially declined the offer and then-Senator Culleton was still looking for a chief of staff when she flew into Melbourne on 11 August 2016. She was there to help him with a meeting he had organised with the ANZ Bank about some farmers whose properties the bank was trying to repossess.

That meeting changed everything for Margaret. They were hostile, she says, downright cruel, even, and if Culleton was going to take his fight to parliament, she decided she was going to be there to help.

The Monday after she arrived in Canberra, Margaret had been working on her employment forms to make her position official and was on the way to the scanner when Culleton's phone rang. Margaret caught his attention and he motioned for her to come in and sit down. Pauline Hanson was on the line and he put her on speaker phone. Turns out, Hanson didn't want Margaret around, either.

'That's fine. *You're* not getting her,' he quipped.

Leaders were supposed to stand by their people, Margaret knew, and any doubts she might have been having about her decision vanished with that one comment and were replaced by questions about Pauline Hanson, Senator for Queensland.

* * *

Margaret Menzel was an odd fit for a One Nation staffer. She was born Margaret Dell'Alba, to Italian parents. Her father had come over from Italy as a migrant in the days of the White Australia Policy and worked in a sugar mill, then as a builder, then as a farmer with his father-in-law. That's how he met Margaret's mother, an Australian-born Italian from an established farming family who had worked land south of Gordonvale.

It was Margaret's grandfather who kept the family on the land during World War II. Italians were already outsiders among the homogeneous communities in Queensland's far north in those days and, when the war broke out, they were the enemy within.

The government had started up a policy of internment for any Italians suspected of working with the other side, and in doing so, their Anglo neighbours saw an opportunity. It was good land the Italians worked, and their English was bad.

All it took was one call to the police and an anonymous tip that an Italian farmer was working with the Japanese to get the cops around there. When the Italian farmer couldn't understand, let alone answer, their questions, he would be interned, leaving their land disused.

One by one, it happened to their neighbours. Instead of letting the land fall into disuse, however, Margaret's grandfather took over the six neighbouring farms and worked himself into the ground to keep them productive, until he too was reported to the police. Someone claimed he was leaving boulders in the fields to signal the Japanese.

Margaret's grandfather was shrewd, though. He knew enough English to get the message and when they came knocking, he took them out to show them the rocks in his fields and told them they were welcome to take them away. They would be doing him a favour. He didn't have the equipment to move them.

It was a kind of racism that Margaret felt while growing up in Gordonvale, long before it was swallowed by Cairns. One day she was out on the street when all the kids in the neighbourhood started to throw stones at her. No one stopped them. No one came to help. The only person who acted was her grandmother, who wrapped her arms around Margaret and sheltered her from the rocks. She remembers looking through her fingers as the blood trickled down.

Maybe it was this experience, maybe it was just her need to make things better, but Margaret became political young. She got involved in student representative councils and went so far as to lobby politicians. That's how she met Bob Katter originally, when she met with him during his time in Joh Bjelke-Petersen's government.

She married into politics in 1981 when she wed Max Menzel, a former cane farmer from Ayr and a member of the Queensland Legislative Assembly for Mulgrave who served from 1980 to 1989. The Menzels were good friends with Katter, Max having served as the president of his party for a time.

Margaret kept on with her activism though she didn't think herself an activist, preferring the word 'advocacy'. On the issues, she cared most about the rights and wellbeing of children. She opposed racism, but she thought something needed to be done about Islam and the kind of violence she heard about overseas. Even the Muslims she had known growing up were scared of it, she said. It was bad for women and bad for gay people as far as she was concerned.

Her main work, though, was to promote those causes dear to the farmers and agricultural workers of her regions, and it was through her work on those issues that she first met Rodney Culleton. It was back around 2014 when three-quarters of Queensland baked under a drought and the red ink flooded farmers' spreadsheets, leaving the debts unpaid. The banks were moving to foreclose on the properties, and farming communities across the state were organising to resist them. This kind of thing had been happening as far back as 2001, Margaret says, and it was all part of 'Agenda 21', a plan by government to force farmers to exit the industry.

In 1992, the UN had passed Agenda 21, a voluntary action plan that was little more than a series of suggestions about how governments at all levels might develop more sustainable communities. Nothing was legally binding about the document, but with time and the internet, it loomed large in the minds of fringe US sovereignty movements. A man called Tom DeWeese had founded a group based in Warrenton, Virginia, called the 'American Policy Center'. It was an exercise in astroturfing, a beige title that gave the privately funded, tax-exempt non-profit a thin veneer of credibility to any passing observer. In turn, DeWeese found a soap-box to churn out increasingly shrill articles pitching Agenda 21 as a direct attack on US sovereignty and a secret socialist plot to undermine property rights.

Slowly, other groups took notice, and eventually the conspiracy hit the big time when Glenn Beck of Fox News gave it oxygen. Beck would go on to write a fiction book titled *Agenda 21*, depicting what he imagined was the end game for those shadowy groups promoting it.

It was all a paranoid delusion, but it still made the jump across to Australia, where Agenda 21 adapted to the local climate as an alleged conspiracy between environmental groups, big banks and world government to undermine the property rights of farmers. It was a way of thinking that framed what Margaret was doing as an advocate, and made sense of the enemy she was trying to fight. As a result of her advocacy, Margaret says the Menzels themselves were targets of legal action by banks that she alleges was designed to bankrupt them.

In Winton, at the farmers' 'Last Stand' rally, Margaret met Culleton. She had been asked to get on the stump to a gathering of farmers there who were fighting to stay on the land. Culleton listened to her speak, and she in turn heard him talk about what was happening to the cattle industry in Western Australia.

Culleton is a big man, with broad shoulders and heavy paws, and he seemed to care. Margaret was impressed. Afterwards she introduced herself to Culleton and talkback radio presenter Alan Jones, and from then on she and Culleton stayed in regular contact.

A parliamentary joint committee on impaired loans and corporations had been scheduled for 16 February 2016 in Sydney, and both Culleton and Margaret were heading there to speak. When the day came and the hearings were open to submissions, they hadn't allowed enough time for Margaret to speak, so she ended up sharing Culleton's time.

Through that process Culleton came to the attention of Pauline Hanson. One Nation had no real machinery in Western Australia and Hanson was looking for a candidate to run, so Culleton first asked Margaret what she thought and Margaret suggested he should go for it.

When he eventually agreed, he asked the Menzels to help run his campaign. Margaret would do the media from Queensland while Max went to work on the ground with Culleton. The first thing they needed, though, was a number two, and Margaret suggested Culleton run with his wife and brother-in-law, Peter Georgiou. Culleton agreed.

To begin with, Max thought Culleton didn't stand a chance. No one knew him and, early on, Hanson and Ashby wanted to target Perth and Bunbury. Max's strategy was to go further out, to hit the areas held by the Nationals. After all, he had been a Nat and knew how things worked in the party. He understood they relied on a natural order being maintained, that so long as the party of the country pointed an accusing finger towards the cities, they never really had to deliver. Anyone who walked in promising to actually do something had the potential to disrupt the status quo.

Hanson and Ashby disagreed. To them it was a waste of resources, but Culleton and Max did it anyway. At first they had no traction, but halfway through the campaign something seemed to shift, and Max sensed a turnaround by the time they pulled into Geraldton.

'My God, the reception we got when we got to Geraldton,' he remembers.

That was when he called Margaret and told her things had changed. Culleton might just win a seat.

Then it came true. It was the first time One Nation had a federal senator in Western Australia, though the Menzels never heard a thank you.

'In Canberra, she said, "I got the candidates elected," but she didn't mention the Menzels, the people who did the work,' Max says.

* * *

The questions Margaret Menzel had about Pauline Hanson began to multiply as parliament went on. During the first week the Senate sat, Attorney-General George Brandis's office held a meet-and-greet with the Senate crossbench. The invite had come from Brandis to Rodney and his chief of staff, and at the bottom he had signed his name 'George'.

Rodney Culleton would have preferred not to go. He didn't warm to the idea of hanging out with a bunch of politicians, but Margaret said he should. If he was going to work with people like Brandis, he would have to build a relationship with them, she reasoned. Culleton saw her point, but agreed to go on the basis that Margaret went along too.

When they arrived, his staff were quick to greet them. Hanson was there, along with Ashby, and the other One Nation senators. Malcolm Turnbull dropped by to say hello and address the room. After him, Pauline spoke, just to say a few words.

'And she said, "Prime Minister, One Nation supports you, tell us what you want us to do,"' Margaret remembers.

One Nation had been elected on a platform that rejected the major parties. In fact, Hanson had named her campaign a 'Fed Up' tour. People didn't want another extension of the major parties, she made clear, they were looking for someone to shake things up, someone to actually represent them. But from day one, Hanson was showing the world that One Nation was here to support the government. Not even the Nationals went that far.

It didn't sit right with Margaret, and there were other things too. In the early days Culleton had baulked against a push by Ashby to vet and review all new hires. There were conflicts between schedules, and on legislation it wasn't clear who was leading what initiative or whether they had any real autonomy to work on an outcome. In one meeting with the prime minister, Hanson had told him One Nation did not support a Royal Commission into the activity of the banks, an integral part of One Nation's 2016 platform. It was a backflip on an issue Hanson had taken to the election and it was the whole reason Culleton was in politics. He considered it a betrayal.

Every One Nation party meeting became a source of friction. When matters came up, there was little discussion; rather, each time, all three of the other One Nation senators would wait for Hanson to arrive and, when she did, she would tell the room how they would vote. Any negotiations that were supposed to be delegated out to each portfolio were overruled. It was top-down leadership, with no information distributed about the legislation they were voting on, what it did, or how it worked.

That was supposed to be the role of Senator Brian Burston. Officially, he was One Nation's Party Whip. It was his job to stay on top of the upcoming votes, the proposed legislation and to ensure that everyone in the party knew which way they were voting on what issues and why.

Every week, all the Senate party whips would meet for a presentation from the government on the bills coming up from the Lower House. At first Margaret ignored the emails collecting in her inbox with the where and when of each meeting. That was supposed to be Burston's responsibility, not hers.

Margaret knew enough to understand that without these meetings, each One Nation senator, and their staff, were flying blind. No one had any idea about the details of what they were voting on or how it worked, meaning that every time one of them spoke to the press, stood up to give a speech or held a meeting, they would be laughed out of the room.

Burston, though, wasn't turning up. Instead he sent his chief of staff, Peter Breen, in his place. And then, eventually, no one at all.

For the minor parties the position of whip was an unpaid, voluntary position, thanks to the arcane rules of the Senate, but that didn't change the fact that someone needed to go. The party could not function properly without the information given at those meetings. Without it, each senator would be forced to chase incomplete details on each new bill that was moving through the Senate by phoning around to some other office, wasting everyone's time in the process. Eventually, it went on so long that Margaret had had enough and told Culleton one evening that he should go.

At first he resisted but Margaret pressed on.

'I can't keep trying to get the information on legislation the hard way,' she told him. 'We need the presentation from each of the major parties to know whether there is something we've missed.'

Only, when Culleton went down to the meeting, they threw him out, saying he wasn't the official party whip.

Back up at the suite, he was furious. It was embarrassing, he said, to be turfed out like that, though Margaret had had a feeling that was going to happen and she waited for the apology call. Sure enough, the office phone rang and the voice on the other end was a staffer from the office of Senator John Williams, the Nationals Senate Whip.

'I'm sorry,' he said, 'I think we just threw your senator out.'

The staffer asked what was going on. Every other whip from every other party was present except One Nation, he said. Margaret explained she had no idea. Burston was the party whip, a federal senator on a starting salary of $199 040 a year, but he apparently wasn't turning up, and the information wasn't flowing through.

The lack of information suited Hanson. She wasn't exactly one to lead by consensus, and whenever it came time for her senators to vote, she wanted them to vote as a bloc. As far as she was concerned, it was her name on the door and her brand that got them elected. If anyone complained, well, that was tough.

* * *

Two months in, Culleton was estranged enough from the party that he was holding quiet meetings with other senators, but it took twice that time for the media to catch on to the tension within One Nation, and then only when someone leaked the story of how James Ashby had thrown his phone at Margaret Menzel.

I knew who leaked the story, and it wasn't Margaret, but when the reporters from *The Australian* came around asking questions, it wasn't her way to lie. She confirmed the exchange and told them about Ashby coming into Culleton's suite, looking to organise a livestream open question-and-answer session through Hanson's Facebook page. It wasn't long after Margaret had been diagnosed with pneumonia and taken a day off.

Margaret wasn't sure about it. Culleton was busy that week, they had been finishing late, and she thought it best to check with him. It wasn't her job to commit the senator to an obligation without running it by him, and she suggested Ashby should put it in writing.

That wasn't what Ashby wanted to hear, though. He wanted it to happen, but the more he insisted, the more Margaret deferred, saying it was Culleton's decision to make. Pretty soon, things turned nasty.

'He said to me, "You're washed up,"' she remembers. '"You're too old. You should go back to the hospital and stay there." Then he repeated it.'

He must have repeated it 'sixteen times', Margaret recalls. To top it off, she was born in February 1958, making her younger than Hanson.

If Margaret was washed up, she wanted to know, what did that make Pauline Hanson?

Ashby apologised by sending a single long-stemmed pink rose and a hand-written thankyou note, but by then it was too late. The story was out. It was a thin edge of a schism that marked the beginning of the end for Rodney Culleton.

* * *

When it was all over, the lonely figure of Rodney Culleton sat forlornly at Aussies Cafe in Parliament House. Life in the Big House went on around him, but he was no longer a part of it. He sat alone in that moment, having been booted from the Senate, stripped of his title, his office, his security pass and his pay cheque. So too had his staff, which was the unfortunate tragedy in the tale of Rodney Culleton.

It was Culleton's complicated relationship with the law that had brought him down. During his time as senator, he was facing the latest in a string of bankruptcy proceedings, personally owing hundreds of thousands of dollars, and facing two separate criminal proceedings.

The first was a theft charge he copped in New South Wales for 11 April 2014 when a tow-truck driver turned up to repossess a truck; a fight broke out and the key was lost. The driver said Culleton stole it. Culleton denied this. A year later, in March 2015, he racked up a second theft charge in Western Australia when it was alleged he stole the key to a hire car used by receivers trying to reclaim the property of a farmer during a solidarity protest organised by other farmers. Culleton claimed he was charged to punish him as a ringleader.

While the bankruptcy proceedings against Culleton hummed in the background and would have ultimately killed his Senate appointment anyway, it was the first of these matters that got Culleton thrown out of office. He had been convicted of theft in March 2016 when he failed to turn up for court in New South Wales and, technically, was awaiting a sentence. The conviction would be annulled that August, but he had already been elected to parliament and so, from the moment the result of the 2016 federal election was called, it started the timer on Culleton's career in politics.

Culleton wasn't the only one. Family First senator Bob Day had been caught up in his own bankruptcy proceedings after his business was taken in a scam and cleaned out. On 7 November 2016 the Senate met to vote on whether or not to refer the two Senators to the High Court. Everyone knew what the result would be, but no one knew what Pauline Hanson was going to say.

'I have always stood for honesty, integrity and what is the truth,' Hanson told the chamber, and from the moment those words escaped her lips, people knew she was throwing Culleton under a bus. She was voting with the majority to send him to the High Court.

'... I know that Senator Culleton will not be too happy with what I have just said. But ... I have fought for eighteen years to be on the floor of this parliament as a representative of the people and I cannot sit back and disregard what may have been a wrong judgement. But I will leave it up to the court to make the final decision.'

With that, Hanson washed her hands of Culleton, and the wounded One Nation senator described having his own people feed him to the lions as an 'ambush'. Not only had One Nation abandoned him, they refused to help with court costs. The party just didn't have the money, Hanson said.

Others in the Senate felt it was unfair. Culleton was a little excitable, but generally well meaning. They suggested he might have a fighting chance if he lawyered up and kept quiet. For good measure, they even put in a few calls to respected constitutional lawyers who might be able to help out.

But then Culleton didn't have the money either. In the lead-up to the High Court referral he had always relied on the advice of his staffer Peter Gargan, a man who had a reputation as a vexatious litigant in four states, a label he wore proudly as a mark of his tenacity. He was not a lawyer; to anyone in that field who knew his name, he was a nuisance who fundamentally misunderstood the role of the legal profession. During his time with Culleton, Gargan had been the author of several wildly incoherent emails that had landed in the inboxes of lawyers, fellow senators, the President of the Senate and court authorities. Each argued, in one way or another, that the entire judicial system and the position of the Governor-General were constitutionally invalid.

Sometimes, these missives were even viewed as an effort to interfere with judicial proceedings. This was the interpretation the Chief Magistrate of Queensland took when a Cairns courthouse received a letter from Culleton's office on behalf of a bankrupt constituent. The letter asked the court to postpone its decision until the constitutional validity of the Australian judicial system was clarified and said Culleton's office would be 'watching with interest'. A second letter was then sent clarifying that the original was not an effort to interfere in court processes.

The matter was referred to police.

When the initial hearings began in the High Court, Culleton appeared self-represented before Chief Justice French. In a long speech, Culleton laid out his belief that the Attorney-General had a vendetta against him. He asked the court to strike out the case and asked that if it proceeded, he should be judged on his character.

The Chief Justice asked him what he was doing about legal representation. Culleton replied that until he was able to 'rehydrate his piggybank' he would be self-represented.

The Chief Justice asked what he thought about the core legal question of the case. Culleton couldn't grasp that the question didn't concern the facts of his criminal trial, but the interpretation of the constitution in this moment. He asked the Chief Justice if they could avoid discussing the constitution. The Chief Justice pointed out it was a constitutional matter.

It was a cringe-worthy exchange that set the tone; though, come December, Culleton had found legal representation after the government eventually agreed to cover the costs. He was on the outs with One Nation, then, and would formally resign from the party on 18 December 2016 to sit as an independent.

As the hearings went on, Bob Katter turned up to support him, making him the only politician to do so. Reporters thought it a cosy relationship between the close-knit cane-farming community, but Katter's presence also served as a show of solidarity, from one farmer to another. It sent a clear message to Hanson: a real leader stands by their people, no matter what.

And when the court handed down its judgement on 3 February 2017, it was short and direct. The High Court held that Culleton had been convicted of a crime at the time of his election, and was awaiting sentencing. Even though his conviction was later annulled, it didn't change the court's opinion that, going by the letter of the law, he had been convicted at that point in time.

Culleton was out, and so was Bob Day after the High Court later ruled that Day had been insolvent at the time of his election. As civilians, both Day and Culleton would be required to repay their salaries, the costs of running their office and the money paid to their staff. Only Day had his debt waived by Special Minister of State Scott Ryan on the basis that he wasn't able to repay it.

The consequences of that decision were swift. Margaret remembers how Bob Day's staff were allowed to stay on in their office after the decision was made. They were there until Day's replacement, Lucy Gichuhi, started giving them a chance to tie off constituent matters and close down the shop. Culleton's staff, meanwhile, were cut off. Their pay stopped coming and their passes were revoked. They packed up the office on their own time, unpaid.

It suggests to Margaret that maybe someone had it in for Culleton, that maybe someone was going after him. Both senators were disqualified and both offices should have been treated the same, though Scott Ryan's people disagree. The two cases were different, they point out. Bob Day resigned when his circumstances became apparent and when the court ruled on his eligibility, the finding was that he had been a senator for part of his term. When judgement day came for Rodney Culleton, the court's view was that he had never been a senator.

Culleton still refuses to accept that. He had been made the same offer as Day in a letter from the Finance Department outlining his options for dealing with the $700 000 debt he owed on office expenses, but at that point Culleton hadn't responded, meaning he was still on the hook. As of 4 July 2017, Culleton still hadn't applied for the waiver and continued to insist that he wouldn't. Accepting the offer would be accepting the High Court's ruling as legitimate. It would mean giving in when Culleton claimed in one letter to have identified 'over 18 Federal and Constitutional laws' which were broken in his removal from office and he intended to protest the injustice at every possible moment. It's why on 6 July 2017, Culleton wrote another long letter to all senators calling for them to act.

It was met with silence.

Margaret, though, still believes in Rodney Culleton, Senator in Exile. 'Of all the One Nation people,' she says, 'he was the one going after the banks by chasing a Royal Commission, and he was getting results.' As far as she's concerned, he was stitched up by George Brandis and thrown to the wolves by Pauline Hanson.

'He's a man of integrity,' Margaret says. 'And they got rid of him because he was too effective.'

Chapter 9

SOCIAL MEDIA KILLED THE RADIO STAR

IT WAS A WEDNESDAY IN EARLY MAY 2017, DOWN IN THE STAFF cafeteria. The tall, lean figure of James Ashby was curled into a couch along with six high-ranking free-to-air television executives who had found their way to him in this part of Parliament House.

They were sitting up the back, and Ashby was dressing down every single one of them in full earshot of anyone who cared to listen.

Pick an issue relating to media and Ashby was giving them a serve. He attacked them for the quality of their coverage and for the concentration of resources in big cities. He attacked them for bias. He attacked them for not keeping enough journalists up in the Top End.

And Pauline Hanson was nowhere to be seen.

It was a monologue that went on for over half an hour, and those listening couldn't believe what they were hearing: here was an advisor to a federal senator publicly scolding television executives. In the world of politics this was a cardinal sin. One Nation may have switched to social media as its primary method of releasing information to its public, but television still beamed the news into the homes of millions of Australians every evening. Either this was the act of an amateur, or it was the mark of a man who no longer gave a damn. People debated which.

That was the trouble with James Ashby, a man people in politics tended to refer to only by his surname. Ever since he had moved onto the national scene, everyone around him had been trying to get a clean read on the guy. Depending on who you asked, Ashby was either a shrewd political genius or a hell-raising hooligan. No one was quite sure what motivated him, or why, which were the first steps in establishing a good working relationship with Pauline Hanson's chief of staff. He controlled complete access to the party leader, so if you wanted to deal with Hanson, you had to deal with Ashby.

That, perhaps, is the way Ashby liked it. The laws of supply and demand gave him enormous power, and the full confidence of Hanson gave him the freedom to do as he wished, a stunning change of fortune for a man who, only two years earlier, had been radioactive.

* * *

James Ashby's parents call him regularly and tell him they hate that he is back in parliament. They hate what it does to him and they wish he had never taken the job with Pauline Hanson. He would be better off back at home with them.

Ashby, at times, agrees with them. He tells people he would rather be somewhere else, anywhere else, than back in parliament. He hates the place, he says, hates the bitter trench warfare that goes on in the hallways. He hates the way people are always probing for vulnerability or leverage, and he hates the way scandal seems to follow him around.

It's something that started in his time before politics. As a young man, midway through his radio career he was fired from a station after clashing with a manager.

The second time it happened, he had threatened a rival radio DJ over the phone. Ashby later said it all began as a joke but was 'taken a little too far and taken a little too seriously'. He soon apologised, though the person at the centre of Ashby's attention didn't want to hear it and, in the end, Ashby couldn't escape a criminal conviction.

If these were minor missteps of a young man, the third time it happened Ashby went big and acted with purpose. In an intricate tale of naked ambition amplified by raw cunning, Ashby found himself caught up in one roaring bastard of a scandal that would bloody two federal governments and the political careers of at least two federal politicians. It was the Peter Slipper Affair, or Ashbygate, depending on who is telling the story: a political black hole, a dark, whirling vortex of shifting allegations and counter-allegations of sexual impropriety and financial irregularities played out under the flash of newspaper cameras. The whole thing tainted the careers of everyone it touched, and was, without a doubt, politics at its dirtiest.

The main character in that story was Speaker of the House Peter Slipper, an ordained minister with a loyal wife and a political career that, during his time in the Liberal Party, had been doomed the moment unseated Liberal MP Mal Brough started to stack branches in Fisher, Slipper's Queensland electorate. Sensing opportunity, the Gillard government offered Slipper an out by giving him the chance to serve as Speaker of the House until the next election, making him a renegade among Tony Abbott's Liberal National Party. In response, Slipper resigned and turned independent, a bold move, but a rational one in an environment where his own party was essentially handing his seat to another.

And when he changed roles, he brought with him the then 33-year-old James Ashby.

Ashby had skills. He understood the power of social media before the rest of politics caught on and he had design experience from his time running a printing business. He seemed to catch Slipper's attention when the politician plucked the openly gay man off the Queensland strawberry farm where he was working and plunged him into the world of federal politics.

The end, or maybe the beginning, came when Ashby filed a sexual-harassment claim against Slipper. The story broke as Ashby was flying home from New York. The sexually explicit messages Slipper had been sending Ashby went public, along with claims Slipper had been abusing his Cabcharge vouchers.

His enemies used it as a way to pin the turncoat, while his supporters claimed Ashby had illegally obtained his diary and shopped it around to other ministers. When it went to trial, Justice Steven Rares of the Federal Court threw out the initial case on the basis it was an abuse of process designed to target Slipper's reputation. That decision was later overturned on appeal by the Full Bench of the Federal Court, though Ashby would later drop the matter saying that the successful appeal confirmed that sexual harassment had taken place.

In the aftermath, everyone walked away bruised. Ashby had been dragged through the mud and left almost bankrupt. Politically, he had made a play, a big one and certainly a risky one, and it had blown up in his face. Slipper, too, was left broken afterwards and Brough, who helped the scandal get off to a flying start, had killed his career. In Ashby's telling, rather than give him up, Brough had resigned.

'If I ever had to go to war, Mal Brough is the guy I want on my side,' Ashby was once heard to say.

Something in Ashby hardened after this. His name and reputation, so carefully cultivated with dreams of one day running for office himself, took a beating. He didn't have the money to run as an independent and there was no way a party would pick him up from that point on. And if, somehow, he did manage to run, every lurid claim and counter-claim would be dug back up and thrown in his face.

Hanson offered redemption – or, rather, opportunity. After the Slipper scandal had died down and Ashby had gone into exile, the pair met when One Nation used Ashby's small printing business in the lead-up to the 2015 Queensland state election. Ashby had called the party offering cheap printing on condition he got to meet Pauline. On Election Day he offered to shoot film for her, and he then began to use his pilot's licence to fly Hanson between regional Queensland towns. The pair spent many hours alone together in the air, and got to know each other well. Both had been dragged through the media, had the indignities of their lives played out on people's TV screens, and been through the courts.

Both had taken a knife to the chest, and both had come away with scars.

Hanson took a liking to the bright young man and brought him into the fold. Ashby later insisted it was by her invitation only. In doing so she offered Ashby a way out of purgatory, and Ashby gave her the input of someone much younger. No one bothered to look into Ashby's background, however, a fact confirmed by a disgruntled Ian Nelson when he was forced out as One Nation treasurer and replaced by Hanson's brother-in-law, Greg Smith. If anyone had thought to run even a quick Google search, Nelson said, no one would have let Ashby loose on the party.

Pauline Hanson had always been a Che Guevara in want of a Fidel. She had the spirit but needed a partner to take care of the nitty-gritty. This partner was almost always male, and the relationship would often turn romantic. Hanson hated when journalists quietly pointed out to her, often out of concern, that this afforded those men undue control over her and her operation. Pauline Hanson was the headline, she insisted. She was the leader. She made her own choices.

None of which made the observation of those journalists who followed her any less true. She had set up her catering business with Morrie Marsden in 1988, but the relationship would eventually become more than business. The same was true of David Oldfield, who managed her campaign during her failed 1998 re-election bid, and who would eventually use Hanson to springboard his own run in New South Wales state politics with a One Nation franchise.

Ashby, though, was different. In public, Hanson referred to him as an 'adopted son' whom she trusted unconditionally. In private, they virtually lived together while in Canberra for parliament, sharing a two-bedroom accommodation.

Their bond was such that, at times, the separate and distinct roles of senator and advisor began to blur, causing confusion among those dealing with Hanson's office, and sometimes even among One Nation staff. No one could be sure in what capacity Ashby was acting, or exactly what authority his word carried.

All people could be sure of was that Ashby was off limits. When One Nation's soldiers started to question his decisions and demand he be put in his place, Hanson refused to fire him.

He was 'too valuable', she said, and that's all she would hear on the matter.

* * *

The name Ashby leaves a poor taste in the mouths of former One Nation staffers, though as far as Ashby was concerned, he was put in the job to professionalise the party. According to the political commentariat, One Nation's rise or fall depended on their ability to 'professionalise' in the way Marine Le Pen, daughter of French fascist Jean-Marie Le Pen, had done for her father's party when she forced him out and took control. For the most part, Ashby had been driving in that direction, only in the process he had run up against a fatal contradiction: a party of the One Nation variety only exists thanks to the dogged individualism of its members and a shared ethic of total defiance. It was always a recipe for chaos.

The first serious problem started when Hanson left Rodney Culleton for dead during the initial challenge to his legitimacy. For Hanson and Ashby, a referral to the High Court was a quick solution to a tiresome problem, but the party's rank and file fumed. They respected a strong leader, but a strong leader, they felt, didn't leave their own people on the field. This had Ashby written all over it, they said.

And then came news of a preference deal with the Liberals out west. That was Ashby's handiwork too, they thought. He was a Liberal, and so was Pauline, once. Now the party was voting with the government 74 per cent of the time, and was doing deals with Liberals who had done them no favours in the past. Everyone remembered 1998 when Hanson was denied a federal seat thanks to the cooperation of the major parties, and they weren't prepared to forgive. As far as the One Nation membership were concerned, Hanson should take no prisoners.

And few could forget how Ashby had demanded access to candidates' social-media accounts and dumped them at a moment's notice for saying something he didn't like – a terrible sin in a party where free speech was supposed to be hardwired into its identity. If the whole point of One Nation was that it defied the left's culture war, the idea that people were being fired for saying something homophobic or misogynistic or 'out there' was met with loathing.

And the party sure was making a lot of mistakes. As the purges started to wash through One Nation's ranks, its former staffers and supporters were only too happy to help reporters find the sore spots. This is how *Four Corners* broke the story that property developer Bill McNee had bankrolled the purchase of a plane, which had not been declared but which was being used by Ashby to taxi Hanson around regional Australia. Labor responded by referring the matter to the Australian Electoral Commission (AEC), and One Nation, in a panic, clung to the line that the plane had been given as a gift personally to James Ashby, despite Hanson having previously said it belonged to the party.

When Ashby and Hanson pushed back, telling journalists that this was a dishonest smear campaign being carried out by disgruntled ex-members such as Ian Nelson, Nelson responded by releasing tapes of their conversations in a bid to defend his character and strike at Ashby.

'Can I just point out,' Ashby said on tape, 'and I've said this before, there is an opportunity for us to make some money on this, if we play it smart. People say you can't make money out of state elections, but you can.'

Ashby emphasised 'you can'.

'And I'll deny I ever said this,' he went on, 'but what stops us from getting a middleman or gracing, ah, like I'm happy to grace in cash double the price of whatever it is. And we say to the candidates, we will fund fifty per cent of this package.'

He emphasised 'package'.

'The package might be five grand, you're going to pay two-and-a-half, and we'll pay the other two-and-a-half of the five. The other two-and-a-half is profit. It's the fat.'

The others in the meeting interjected. They tried telling Ashby that the candidates didn't have much money to begin with and that it was a bad idea, but Ashby cut them off by suggesting a way to get the money back through Electoral Commission Queensland.

In another part of the recording, Ashby can be heard outlining a plan to buy corflutes for five dollars and on-sell them to party candidates for eleven dollars.

There was a brief moment of uncomfortable silence.

'That's what the Liberal Party do,' Ashby says.

'We're not the Liberal Party,' came the response from another in the meeting.

When the tapes hit the news, Hanson and Ashby responded by presenting a united front. Hanson said she had killed the idea then and there, and Ashby said it was a regrettable choice of words. In doing so they took aim at Ian Nelson and former staffer Saraya Beric, accusing them of carrying out a vendetta.

Nelson in turn released a second tape, of a phone call between himself and Hanson in which she had just learned someone had named Bill McNee to a reporter as the generous One Nation party donor.

'Who knows Bill's name?' she asked Nelson. 'No one. We always kept it very, very quiet. Who knows that he paid the money up-front for the office? No one knew. There was the four of us. That's it. It was tight-knit.'

It was not the only story that broke. The *Saturday Paper* published an investigation into the corporate structure of One Nation, which forced through a reorganisation in November 2016, leaving it with a non-compliant constitution. It was dry story, one that lacked the theatre of leaked audio recordings and required a certain degree of legal literacy to work through, but the gist was that it looked like the party had defrauded its members and, if that was true, could face deregistration.

For a guy like Ashby, who worked eighty hours a week and had a reputation as a slick operator, he was playing it fairly loose. He had a genius for political positioning, like when entrepreneur Dick Smith gave a qualified endorsement of One Nation's immigration policies and Ashby made sure it was heard from coast to coast, knowing the public would soon forget Smith's heavy caveat.

Only when it came down to working the internal machinery of the party, Ashby struggled to manage those human relationships. Which was a problem. Politics, after all, is a deeply human activity.

But then, none of this came as a surprise to those who knew James Ashby.

He had nothing to lose.

Chapter 10

PREFERENTIAL TREATMENT

GLENN DRUERY IS SITTING IN THE QANTAS CLUB EATING greens and broccoli salad and is happy to talk One Nation, he says, though he's going to keep eating. He's heading to Colorado for a holiday, and his flight leaves in twenty minutes.

As far as political operatives go, Glenn Druery is a man of myth and colourful metaphors. These days he serves as Derryn Hinch's chief of staff, but mostly he's known for his work as the Australian electoral system's arms dealer.

Druery first got into the game in 1996 when he co-founded the Outdoor Recreation Party, a middle-of-the-road environment party, and ran as a candidate at the 1999 New South Wales state election. Going into that race, Druery had picked up a copy of psephologist Antony Green's analysis of the 1995 state election and then weaponised it. At the New South Wales election in '99, the 'Minor Party Alliance' was born in an election that saw a total of 264 candidates for 81 groups run for the Upper House.

Druery had caught onto the idea that cooperation was often better than competition when it came to the smaller players. The Alliance was forged as a way to coordinate the flow of preferences to help elect outsiders who ordinarily would have no chance. The idea was that no matter the specific policies they were pursuing, no matter if they were left, or right, or where they stood on the social issues, everyone involved cooperated to maximise their chances of getting into office.

As far as Australian politics went, it had never been done before and almost everyone was surprised at the result. Though Druery himself wouldn't be elected, his man, Malcolm Jones, polled just 7264 votes, or 0.2 per cent, rounded, and still made it over the line, along with several Minor Party Alliance candidates. Jones would later resign in disgrace after finding himself the subject of an ICAC investigation, but that didn't change the result.

'If I was building a bomb, to blow up a bridge, I created a nuclear weapon. I didn't realise how effective it was going to be,' says Druery. 'If I was playing derivatives, I would be a millionaire.'

When the media worked out what happened, they started calling Druery the 'preference whisperer'. It's a label he had no part in creating, he insists, but it laid the groundwork for a mythology that would be good for business as a freelance political strategist. The major parties had their own tacticians and strategists who studied the numbers and analysed all possible outcomes for each election to give the party bosses the best shot at electoral success. Until Druery, they simply had a monopoly, and as much as public figures among the major parties railed against the latest marriage of free enterprise, expertise and politics, the only thing that surprised insiders was that it had taken someone so long to work out they could make a buck doing it.

From the start, One Nation was out. Druery had met Brian Burston in the early days and took an immediate dislike to the man. Burston was 'unintelligent', he thought, and couldn't understand what Druery was trying to achieve. To top it off, One Nation was racist, and that crossed a line. Equal opportunity might have been the golden rule of the 'Minor Party Alliance', but One Nation became the exception. When the ballots were counted at that election in '99, Druery kept Burston out of office.

From then on, Druery says, he waged a quiet, one-man war against Pauline Hanson's One Nation, which marginalised the party. At One Nation's 2013 revival, when Hanson re-entered politics, Druery says, he joined with Ian Nelson and Jim Savage to convince Hanson to run in New South Wales rather than Queensland, where, he told her, her chances for re-election were better. In reality, he used One Nation to harvest their votes and redirect them elsewhere, a strategy that he says worked until 2016 when Malcolm Turnbull changed the voting rules to keep someone like him from working the system. As if that wasn't enough, the government had called a double dissolution – and that, in Druery's view, is the only reason One Nation is back.

Druery's cold war turned hot in March 2017 when Brian Burston gave a speech on the floor of the Senate under the protection of parliamentary privilege. Burston complained that Druery had called the One Nation offices threatening to 'tear out Pauline Hanson's throat' if she didn't cooperate on preferences. Burston called Druery's system of preference harvesting a 'charade' and a 'pyramid scheme' and said he felt compelled to call Druery out in parliament because there was nowhere else he could take his complaints.

As far as politics goes, it was a dirty move. Burston used privilege to smear Druery's character free from the threat of a defamation lawsuit and the need to prove his claims in court. As soon as Burston's speech hit the news, Druery started to get calls from reporters asking if he wanted to hit back – and he obliged. He promised open warfare on One Nation, pledging to bleed them of preferences trench by trench, state by state, first in Queensland, then South Australia and then Victoria.

'It was a strategically stupid thing to do,' Druery says of Burston's speech. 'If you read his speech, if you take the time to look between the lines of his speech, it's a desperate, scared, failed man, and by the way, when he delivered the speech, he was shaking. Burston is scared of me, he doesn't understand what I do, and he sure as shit can't stop me.

'Many people in the media think Pauline Hanson's some sort of electoral Harry Potter,' he says. 'But her future is mapped out, it's planned out. Hanson is like the political equivalent of the dotcom bubble in the late nineties.

'If I sound cocky, I am cocky. Someone's got to stand up to these people.'

Chapter 11

EXPERTS

RICHARD DENNISS WAS IN SYDNEY ON THE DAY OF THE US Presidential election, sitting in a taxi on the way back to Canberra and his job as Chief Economist at the Australia Institute when the news came in that Donald Trump had won.

Like everyone else, he was surprised. Economics was his game, not American politics or electoral polling, and the people he had spoken to in the lead-up to Election Day had all said the same thing: the billionaire real-estate developer with zero experience in politics had no chance of winning.

Thinking back, Denniss says he should have seen the result coming. Donald Trump was marching on the White House, that was plain to see; but then, hindsight is always twenty–twenty. What he did notice was that as soon as the pollsters he had been speaking to were proved wrong, they started to tell him how the polls aren't always as accurate as they used to be.

'Anyone who thinks they know what is going to happen in an election is exaggerating their foresight,' he says.

Richard Denniss may be an economist, but one of his areas of expertise is the sketchy way other experts have been doing business over the past two decades. Whether it's academic guns for hire, or politicians cherry-picking data while running critical voices out of town – Denniss has watched the value of knowledge in public debate be slowly whittled away.

'It's hard to run democracy, it's hard to run capitalism, it's hard to run a bowling club without expertise,' Denniss says. 'It makes sense that we'd want to defer to experts for some of that, so we trust them.

'We've debased the notion of experts when anyone waving data around is treated evenly. It used to be shameful if a professor called out a politician for using data wrongly. Now when you've got some politician waving some numbers around and a professor who has worked in the field for thirty years saying that's inappropriate, we call it a draw.'

Once upon a time, it was government departments and Treasury that had a monopoly on expertise in the world of public policy. It was their job to develop policy, evaluate the ideas of outsiders and supply the expertise that underpinned them.

That changed from the 1980s as the Australian economy began to financialise so that every aspect of life, from the houses people raised families in to their retirement nest egg, became a commodity to be traded. In this way economics became the bottom line in every conversation about what to do, starting with Paul Keating's 'big picture'.

This process even commoditised experts and expertise. As governments slashed or starved public spending and invited the private sector to play a deeper role in handling everything from the administration of welfare services to consultations over environmental compliance, those whose job it was to advise governments started to make money advising corporations. There were dollars to be made selling expertise to the highest bidder, and everyone from tobacco companies to the mining industry brought in their own experts.

Today, Denniss says, Australia is the world's biggest spender on economic modelling. An intellectual labour that used to be the sole domain of Treasury can now be bought from any number of independent consultants who worked out they can make a killing writing inch-thick documents for mining companies looking to sell an open-cut mine to local communities and their elected representatives.

* * *

In the same way uranium can be used to generate power or build the kind of bombs that end debates, the spreadsheets that once were used to understand complex relationships between trends now are used to win arguments. A corporation or industry body willing to drop a cool million on a campaign could force a complete U-turn in public policy. Oil and gas companies did it with climate change by funding climate-sceptic groups and in Australia mining companies did it with the mining tax. Lately, it has been the banking and financial sector making thinly veiled threats to push back against any government moves to tax their industry.

That is how the spreadsheet became weaponised. Ever since, most public debates turned into conversations about maths, where expertise, or knowledge, became the method to force through favourable outcomes rather than understand trends and make better decisions. As the monetary value of this work increased, the inherent value of expertise was cheapened.

'And it's not just modelling, it's facts and data,' says Denniss.

An example is national gross domestic product (GDP) figures. In March 2017, the headlines of every news organisation in the country ran good news for the government: Australian GDP figures for the previous quarter had just been released showing the country had grown, marking twenty-six years of uninterrupted economic growth. On every news channel commentators hailed the development as a sign that everything was as it should be and the doomsayers were proved wrong. The economy had grown and all that 'economic anxiety' people had been talking about was little more than misplaced emotion.

Problem was, GDP figures, as a national average, don't recognise regional variations and are driven by internal mechanisms that are never discussed in any real detail. It's a similar story with each month's unemployment figures: each tick up, each tick down is closely studied as an indication of the overall health of the economy, but the actual value of these measures is lost.

'When you watch the news at night, they tell you what the temperature is in the city you live in,' says Denniss. 'We never tell you what the average temperature was in Australia today, because no one cares what the average temperature was in Australia today. When it comes to GDP or unemployment figures, we talk about national averages. We don't talk about unemployment in your region, [or] growth in your region.'

A similar problem exists when it comes to talking about what's happening with wealth inequality. It's impossible to talk about the issue without numbers, but depending on who you ask, which spreadsheets they are using, how they are calculating it and what questions they ask in the process, making sense of it can be tricky, especially given that the two landmark studies of wealth and income inequality appear to contradict each other.

The first is the Melbourne Institute's 2017 HILDA (Household, Income and Labour Dynamics in Australia) survey, a long-term study of more than 17000 people that started in 2001 and has been looking at their incomes ever since. That study found very little change in income inequality, and in doing so seemed to contradict the Australian Bureau of Statistics (ABS) which had surveyed 27000 people every year since 1981 and, according to the latest data available at the time of writing, found that income inequality has been increasing.

Each study has its uses depending on what kind of political argument you want to make. Neither really paints a good picture of what is going on because income inequality is only one half of a problem that also includes the concentration of wealth in Australian society.

On that score, the ABS data showed a growing concentration of wealth among the country's richest. In 2003–2004, the wealthiest 20 per cent of Australia held 58.6 per cent of total household wealth, while the poorest 20 per cent held just 1.4 per cent. A decade later that figure had increased, with the wealthiest 20 per cent holding 61 per cent of total household wealth, while the poorest 20 per cent had shrunk to just 1 per cent.

On these figures, the Gini coefficient was calculated, which is a way of working out what is going on across a whole national economy. The closer the number moves towards zero, the more equal a society is. On wealth inequality, that number for the 2003–2004 period began at 0.573 and moved up to 0.605 as of 2013–2014, showing that the rich had gotten richer. Meanwhile, the ABS Gini calculation for income inequality was 0.333 in 2013–2014, compared to 0.32 in 2011–2012, showing that the poor had stayed about the same. To put that in a global perspective, in 2014 the OECD pegged Australia's Gini coefficient for income inequality at 0.0337 compared to 0.394 in the United States.

Among the blizzard of numbers, technicalities and political spin that come with any discussion of wealth inequality are all the other smaller independent studies produced by groups of researchers, think tanks, demographers and international bodies, each variously motivated by different politics, academic scope, commercial interest or government mandate. This is how a debate that has raged overseas, where data collection methods are not as good, arrived in Australia with a bang.

It's an aspect of the debate that Professor Peter Whiteford of the Australian National University (ANU) says is not particularly useful if you want a more complete picture of what is happening in Australia. Few people outside the close-knit world of economists and political advisors sit around wringing their hands over each tick up or down of the unemployment rate, and few people think about the numbers on wealth and income inequality when they go into the polling booth. The way it plays out is more instinctive than that, more a feeling that people are being left behind.

'I think the labour market story is a lot more gloomy,' Professor Whiteford says, before going on to explain how that's a story about the loss of good jobs, insecure work and a growing underclass.

'Let's define a good job as somebody who is in full-time work and isn't low paid, where the standard is if you are paid two-thirds of the median income or more,' Professor Whiteford says. 'You can call these "good jobs". What you then get is all the people who are not in the labour force, who are not employed, who are part-time employed, or even if they're full-time employed but they're low paid. When you look at that from the years 1978 to 2016 the proportion of men with good jobs fell from 71 per cent to less than 56 per cent, which is a massive change.'

In that time, Professor Whiteford says, more people have become educated, and more women are landing 'good jobs', while a high proportion of the jobs going around are high-skilled and concentrated in major cities. This is good news for some, but anyone caught on the other side of it struggles. In a world where education and wealth define success and social position, it's the people caught working low-skilled jobs or in low-paying fields such as aged care, retail or hospitality, and those who never finished high school, who react first.

All of this is how people living in a place like Elizabeth, South Australia – where nearly one in five people across the council area are unemployed – may hear talk about how the country has gone twenty-six years without a recession, or how Australia nationally is running at 5.9 per cent unemployment in March 2017, and quite reasonably shrug.

When that person looks around the dinner table and grasps how everyone in their family is on welfare, or can't find more than a low-paid casual job, it doesn't take a master's degree to see the trend. In a nation with a never-ending thirst for data, where the quantitative has triumphed over the qualitative so thoroughly, it is those who are stagnant who react first. Those with the least education are often the first to know something is wrong, even if they don't have the words, or the spreadsheet, to describe what it is. Telling them everything is getting better overall is meaningless to them and quoting national GDP figures at people in that kind of environment does nothing to change their circumstances. All it does is deny their direct lived experience in favour of the national average, ignoring the regional variations and quirks which define people's lives and, in the process, it turns expertise into a class issue. In the end, those whose job it is to crunch the numbers find their credibility eroded while those on the bottom rung become vulnerable to anyone ruthless enough to make political capital out of beating up the voice of reason.

This is how Bernie Sanders and Donald Trump could get away with claiming that the unemployment figures were flat-out wrong. Of the two Trump was far more aggressive, claiming that the 'real unemployment rate' in the United States was not 5.2 per cent in August 2015, but somewhere in the region of 20 per cent, or even as high as 42 per cent. It was a lie, but *The Australian* picked up the theme when it ran an editorial by its economics correspondent Adam Creighton in May 2017 titled: 'Be honest about unemployment – it's above 15 per cent'.

At that time, *The Australian* had been trying to use data to get a better picture of the economic health of the nation.

Even as it published an editorial by David Uren denying that wealth inequality was rising in Australia, *The Australian* was using tax returns and welfare figures to identify those regions around the country that were receiving more in welfare than they paid and in doing so highlighted those regions that have been hit by de-industrialisation, inter-generational disadvantage and localised recession.

It was against this backdrop that Creighton's editorial appeared. Creighton didn't discuss the limits of statistical measures, or even the need to combine this information with other information to get a clearer idea of what is happening in the economy. Instead he attacked the very credibility of the ABS, accusing it of lying, despite its use of the International Labour Organisation standard measure for collecting unemployment data, one that is recognised and deployed worldwide.

Rather than using the data provided by the ABS to explore those wealth divides and talk about the bigger issues, the experts took another beating.

* * *

When Michael Gove, then the UK's Justice Secretary, said in a live, one-on-one interview during the heat of the Brexit debate that 'people have had enough of experts', the world gasped. The reaction was instant. The interview was played over and over. In one move, Gove appeared to have rejected a cornerstone of the Enlightenment, and the basis for evidence-based policy.

Gove was then followed by Trump, whose entire presidential campaign seemed to defy every single rule by which the objective media lived. Trump didn't know. He *felt.* To Trump, something just had to feel true to be true and this is how he won: a fuzzy *truthiness* delivered with conviction that made it feel real to anyone watching. He exaggerated unemployment figures and illegal-immigration numbers. He inflated the size of the crowd at his inauguration and the number of people watching the ceremony on television. He claimed to have won the most Electoral College votes since Ronald Reagan was in the White House. All of these were false, but the list kept growing. Every speech, every communication was a catalogue of lies.

As with Gove, the horror set in and everyone struggled to find a way to respond. *Rolling Stone* journalist Matt Taibbi captured the overall mood when he pointed out that truth was supposed to be off-limits.

'Facts are the closest thing we have to a national religion,' Taibbi wrote. 'In America, where sex-tapers become royalty and monster trucks massively outdraw Shakespeare, even advertisers aren't supposed to just lie. The truth is the last thing here that isn't openly for sale.'

Trump's lies however, served a tactical purpose in that they helped him tap into the anger and paranoia of his base, and that was all he needed.

Trump, though, was just the biggest, loudest voice engaging in 'post-fact' or 'post-truth' politics. This took the post-modern idea that 'truth' was the sum of all known facts with a line drawn through the middle, and turned it into a political weapon. All politicians throughout modern history have picked up a whiteboard marker and drawn their own line through all known facts, emphasising some more, others less so, and then coming up with reasons why theirs was a more accurate average than that of their opponents. The key point of difference was that everyone generally worked with the same dots.

This was the post-modern idea of truth, first expressed as a way for powerless people to push back against the powerful, to help create some understanding about how it was that their experience of the world was never heard on the news. Those like Trump and Gove took the idea and put it to work in service of the powerful. On some instinctual level, Gove and Trump understood that the person holding the whiteboard marker could also add or subtract dots at will, and then redraw the line as they pleased. That, after all, was the very definition of power.

While the developed world struggled to come to terms with this, Australia had seen it all before. Before Trump and Gove ever found political success by injecting their personal reality directly into public debate to get ahead, Pauline Hanson was pioneering post-fact politics Down Under as early as 1996.

Pauline Hanson was post-truth, before post-truth. She didn't know. She *felt*. She didn't learn, she assimilated knowledge by talking to people around her. When she ran for office, she would repeat whatever people told her about Aboriginal land rights or the Asian Invasion for the television cameras, which would then stream it into the homes of every Australian around the country. Her speeches were a string of meaningless factoids and empty symbolism. Her ideas, like the Two Per Cent Flat Tax, were hollow, and if actually carried out would hurt the people she claimed to represent. Hanson created for herself, and for her supporters, a false reality so twisted and incoherent, journalist Margo Kingston could barely stomach it by the end of Hanson's 1998 election campaign and could only cope with the stress by chain-smoking outside the venues where Hanson was speaking.

But it was Tony Abbott, Hanson's old sparring partner, who took post-truth into the mainstream and ran with it further than she ever could. Even before he took the Prime Minister's office, his primary target was climate change, which he once described in a speech to a meeting of Victorian Liberal Party members as 'crap'. Even if climate change was happening, he argued in his manifesto *Battlelines*, the consequences weren't knowable and this, in his view, made it insane to do anything to try to stop it.

So he waged a bitter war against the carbon tax and showed his colours in a telling moment at a community forum captured by Peter Hartcher in his book *The Sweet Spot*, which would foreshadow exactly how the man would treat facts and evidence when he took power.

At that meeting, Abbott had taken a question on climate change from someone in the audience asking which of the experts he would listen to on the issue.

'The public,' he answered. 'In a democracy, in the end the people are sovereign.'

He then went on to call for a 'people's revolt' against the government's plan to introduce a carbon tax.

As prime minister, Abbott immediately went to work unpicking every policy Australia had put together on renewable energy and climate change over the previous ten years, while any critical expert who might convincingly contradict the notion that a particularly wet winter disproved climate change soon found their funding under threat, or stripped entirely.

Education was the next target. When the government delivered its 2014 budget, it slashed funding across the board on the basis of 'tightening the belt' and making 'sacrifices'. This had the effect of draining funding from education and any higher-level research that the government considered too 'abstract' while a big boost was given to medical research. At the same time, Abbott offered public funding to Danish economist Bjørn Lomborg, who accepted human-caused climate change was real, but used a cost-benefit analysis to argue that it was pointless to do anything about it. Abbott denounced lawsuits against mega-mines as 'lawfare' and lobbied hard to keep the Great Barrier Reef from being listed as 'in danger'. Abbott even went as far as to claim his repeal of the carbon tax in July 2014 would create two million jobs over ten years in a then workforce of 11.6 million people.

It was bunk, and so too was the 'budget emergency' Abbott used to take down Kevin Rudd, then Julia Gillard, then Rudd again while in Opposition. It was this emergency he used to justify an austerity budget that cut funding for basic services right across the board, despite promising on the eve of the 2013 federal election not to do so in a now-infamous SBS interview. Anyone who made the point that managing the federal budget was nothing like balancing a household budget was denounced as a leftie living in an ivory tower.

And when the crisis became inconvenient, it went away, despite the very real questions that started to be asked as the level of government debt grew.

The label 'post-truth politics' didn't really have currency then. Abbott's critics called him a liar, while his supporters didn't quite know what to make of the situation. Then again, labelling the problem wasn't necessary. Everyone could see where it was going. By the end, the public had tuned out, and even Abbott's own party stopped listening when they saw what was happening in the polls.

And on the day he was removed as prime minister, Abbott found the limit of post-truth politics: the point where a personal reality collides with the hard edge of public office.

Chapter 12

BIG HAT

THE PHONE CALL CAME UP FROM THE SENATE CHAMBER SAYING that the boss was next to speak and needed a stack of documents, now.

I was up in the suite, sleeves pushed up to my elbows like I had been working with my hands, no jacket, no tie. The documents were on the desk, they said, and the others could be found online.

It took me a few minutes to dig out what I needed from the pile of paperwork on another advisor's desk and I ripped the rest from the printer before making the walk down to the Chamber, taking a shortcut through the courtyard.

It was peaceful in those courtyards. You could hear birds, and the sunshine filtered down through the trees and onto the grass, and the faint smell of tobacco would drift across from the smokers' section in one corner where the security guards, cleaners, baristas and staffers would mingle.

As I approached the Chamber I remembered something about how you weren't supposed to enter without a jacket and tie, but there was no time for formalities. I nodded to the security guard outside the Chamber and pushed open the door just enough to slip through. As it pulled open there came a rubbery crack as the noise-cancelling seal broke, and everything went from quiet to booming in a matter of millimetres.

It was a roar, something powerful and violent, yet directed with purpose. From where I stood, it looked like all seventy-six seats had been filled, and at that moment it was One Nation senator Malcolm Roberts's turn to speak.

He stood silhouetted against rows of faces, all eyes fixed firmly on him. He seemed to be giving a speech, or maybe asking a question, and he was using the time to rail against 'the global elites'. He said something that I didn't quite catch, but the Chamber understood, and another roar erupted, this time louder than the first.

I can't remember what day it was. I can't remember what was being discussed. I've tried to find out. I've combed through Hansard and watched replays of video recordings, but I still can't find that moment.

Even if I could, watching it again on television could never capture the feeling of standing at the foot of the Senate that day. This was politics, stripped of its petty rivalries and pedantic ceremonies. It was something raw and honest in a world where those qualities were hard to come by, and harder to measure with any real certainty.

* * *

Malcolm Roberts always struck me as deeply lonely. He is a short man, no taller than five feet, with ice-blue eyes. He would always smile or nod, and when I was getting something to eat or escorting someone through the building, I would see him standing by himself, pacing in a line, mobile phone pressed to his ear and other hand on his hip, engaged in a very serious-looking conversation, with no one else around.

His whole political career was an accident of historical circumstances. As a figure, he had come along at just the right time, to meet just the right people who offered him access to a platform on the national stage. Much like One Nation itself, that was all he needed to get stuck in. Now he was in the spotlight, and he was using every opportunity to take down the scientists and climate-change activists he despised.

Just like all the other high-ranking officers of One Nation, Malcolm Roberts was also a walking contradiction. Politically he was a libertarian, in the American sense, but in a speech he later gave to a conference for the Australian Industry (AI) Group in Canberra on 1 May 2017, Roberts claimed One Nation was a workers' party, and the successor to 'Old Labor'.

'We describe ourselves as a popular nationalist party, but what this means in practice is that we are a predominantly working-class nationalist party – what some may call a "right wing" workers' party,' he said.

'What makes us a "workers' party" is that the membership and support base of One Nation is made up of often poorly paid, hardworking Aussies whose basic decency, quiet patriotism, strong moral compass and fierce work ethic define them as the heart and soul of our nation.

'The fact that One Nation is a working-class party is directly reflected in the backgrounds of our political representatives. Of the four One Nation senators, one was a boilermaker [Brian Burston], one was an electrician [Peter Georgiou], one was a coal miner [Senator Roberts] and one was a fish-and-chip-shop owner [Senator Hanson].'

From there it was a long, meandering history lesson. When it wrapped the reaction was swift, with Labor senator Anthony Chisholm using Twitter to tell Roberts the only workers One Nation represented were the rednecks Labor had long since cut loose.

'Only the old racist element m8 and it's all yours,' Chisholm posted.

In one move Chisolm had flagged the withdrawal of the left–progressive side of politics from the working-class communities they used to represent, instead of hitting Roberts where it hurt: the bold claim to a working-class identity by a guy who spent only three years of his career as a coal-face miner, and the rest in management.

Malcolm Roberts started life as the son of a mine manager in West Bengal, India, after the end of the British Raj. His parents had met while his father was visiting Queensland; Roberts senior married a local girl and took her out to the subcontinent to live with him while he managed a coal mine. Young Master Malcolm wanted for nothing in those days. His driver was Muslim and so was the butler, and the rest of the staff were a mix of Hindu and Buddhist servants.

Roberts doesn't like to talk about this part of his life. It's something that would come back to haunt him in July 2017 when questions started to get raised about the citizenship status of Australia's politicians and whether Roberts's own status possibly violated Section 44 of the Constitution.

Roberts would go on to deny that he was a British citizen, but when the issue dragged on into August, Pauline Hanson would ask the Senate to refer Roberts's case to the High Court. Few argued.

As far as Roberts is concerned, his story began in the period when his father moved the family to the Hunter Valley in New South Wales to manage another mine. What his father did fascinated him, and as a ten-year-old Roberts built replica mining pits in the backyard. He took such a liking to the work, he graduated university in 1977 with a degree in mining engineering and threw himself into a sixteen-year career in the coal industry. Despite his energy and enthusiasm for the positivity culture of self-help gurus and far-eastern spirituality, his career was pockmarked with disappointment. In 1988, he had been managing a mine for Coal & Allied in West Wallsend, New South Wales that failed due to its location. Picking himself up, he left for the United States to undertake an MBA at the University of Chicago; he also got married in the USA and then came back in 1990 as a 35-year-old to manage the Gordonstone Mine, at the time the biggest underground mine in the world. He lasted three years in the job. According to Roberts, the company sided with the union in an industrial dispute, and he left on principle. Others say it was costs overruns that drove him out.

It was a holiday to the Whitsundays with his wife that changed everything. Roberts had turned on the television in his hotel room to find Al Gore's documentary *An Inconvenient Truth* playing, and what he saw hit like a gut-punch for a man who had spent his life in the coal industry. He picked through the film, frame by frame, and began his long crusade against the science of climate change.

The conclusion of that crusade was the publication of his manifesto, *CSIROh!*, a masterpiece in self-delusion. It was a 300000 word treatise, with twenty separate appendices, one 135 pages long. In it, Roberts sewed together a wide array of internet-based conspiracy theories into one hulking Frankenstein's monster of a document. He quoted 'investigative reporter' Daniel Estulin's allegation that Barack Obama is an international drug trafficker. Twice he cited Infowars, an online factory for conspiracy theories such as how Barack Obama was planning to use biological weapons against his own people, or how millions of undocumented workers had been allowed to vote in the 2016 US presidential election. The kicker was that Roberts's main thesis, that climate change is a conspiracy being pushed by the United Nations (UN) and a group of influential banking families, had been lifted uncritically from Eustace Mullins, a vicious anti-Semitic American Holocaust denier, and his book *The Secrets of the Federal Reserve*, one of the most influential anti-Semitic books ever written. According to the *New York Times*, Osama bin Laden kept a copy in the library at his Abbottabad compound.

It was in those years that Roberts spent floating around the internet, working on his manifesto, that he had a brief flirtation with the 'sovereign citizen movement', a group who believe they can declare themselves independent of government authority through a creative use of grammar, and formed a politics that was increasingly libertarian.

Roberts would have lived and died as little more than a slightly annoying yet relatively painless product of the internet were it not for Pauline Hanson. Around the time he published his manifesto, Hanson called him to ask advice on climate change when Ian Plimer, a geologist and climate-change denier once cited by Tony Abbott as an expert disagreeing with climate change, had fallen ill. Roberts stepped up, marking the start of an alliance that would see him run on Pauline Hanson's senate ticket, landing in federal parliament with just 77 first-preference votes and Hanson's leftovers.

Roberts, to his credit, has never forgotten this and remains grateful to the woman who had lifted him up from the obscure fringe to the nation's parliament. During his maiden speech, he made it a point to express his deepest gratitude to his leader.

'Our Pauline, the people's politician,' he said, is a 'woman of great courage.

'Pauline listens to understand, and is honest, courageous and persistent.'

Hanson was caught on camera rolling her eyes at the over-the-top tribute from the number two on her ticket, though she would later claim through social media she had just been embarrassed.

Roberts's other contribution to One Nation was to accelerate the group's growing libertarian influence. He hired into his office the cagey figure of David Goodridge, founder of the anti-government, anti-tax Australian Tea Party. In his speeches Roberts repeatedly outlined a vision of the world that reduced every bill or social issue to a zero-sum choice between a perceived increase in government control, or a perceived increase in personal freedom. When Trump won the US election, Roberts flew the Gadsden flag at parliament, a symbol of the US libertarian movement that has a rattlesnake printed against a yellow background above the words 'Don't tread on me'. In the Senate, he gave a speech hailing Trump's win as 'the beginning of the Western spring', a reference to the Arab Spring that toppled autocratic regimes across the Middle East.

But climate change was always Roberts's main game, and he approached the subject more like a lawyer, forensically working his way through any evidence that came his way supporting the idea humanity was slow-cooking the planet. His goal was not scientific inquiry so much as to introduce as much doubt as possible, while inoculating himself against contradictory evidence by invoking the great cover-up by NASA and the UN whenever challenged.

Of them all, Roberts was the One Nation representative most likely to front the cameras and talk to journalists, even if it was motivated by a desire to use every bit of air time to spread the word and attack NASA or the CSIRO or whichever climate-change activist had his attention at the time. His breakout moment came when he challenged celebrity British scientist Professor Brian Cox on ABC TV's *Q&A* in a disastrous showdown for the senator, when it turned out Cox had prepared for the exchange by bringing along graphs to back up his points.

Cox, like everyone else, could see the pattern. It was like a law of physics: the longer a speech or a conversation with Malcolm Roberts went on, the greater the likelihood that he would talk about 'the climate-change conspiracy', or the benefits of the 'oil and gas sector'. In one case from June 2017, Roberts stood to speak about the Greens' Stop Adani Bill and lurched into a discussion about how the coal sector had saved the lives of thousands of whales. 'Not only do the whales thank coal, not only do the forests thank coal but humanity itself thanks coal,' he said. This kind of thing happened so often, advisors working in or around the Chamber started to take odds on how far into a speech it would happen.

In March 2017, Roberts had also shown the limitations of an outsider candidate when he tried to introduce an amendment to the Fair Work Amendment, a private members bill put up by the ALP. When Roberts tried to amend the bill an objection was raised and he was denied.

In that situation, the general procedure is to move to suspend standing orders and call a debate on the amendment to try to give it some legs. Malcolm Roberts didn't do this. He didn't know he could, didn't know how and nor did any of his staff. One Nation as an entity struggled to attract the kind of talent that understood Senate procedure, tending to hire for ideological purity and personal loyalty rather than professional disinterest and procedural insight. This meant no one seemed to have the initiative or imagination to seek out a musty tome on the subject, or to even call in back-up from the Table Office or Procedure Office, the non-partisan Senate support staff whose very job is to help in that exact situation.

It takes discipline and patience to master the procedural weaponry of parliament, but One Nation didn't have the capacity for it. That was insider stuff. The stuff of the elite. And it was painfully tedious. It was much easier to talk big on the floor of the Senate, make a bit of noise, and maybe get a run on the news that night.

So, Senator Malcolm Roberts, who was taking home $199 040 a year plus staff and expenses as a representative of the people of Queensland, sat down.

Quietly.

Chapter 13

KINGMAKERS

TONY WINDSOR APOLOGISES FOR THE BAD RECEPTION. OUT his way it's so patchy that if he walks from one side of his house to the other, the whole thing drops out.

Ever since he quit politics for health reasons, and failed in his comeback bid, Windsor has been back on the land. In the twenty-two years he served in politics he quit smoking and grew to miss working with the soil. A one-way trip to the capital in those days started with a 300-kilometre drive to the airport, and in Canberra he was a kingmaker, a rebel and a peacemaker. He knew what it was to be hated and feared and respected, all at once.

It was a rough ride in some parts, but Tony Windsor enjoyed the life. That's the funny thing about politics: once you're in its orbit, the gravity is so strong you never really reach escape velocity. While he quit in 2013 due to bad health, Windsor ran again in 2016 after Barnaby Joyce, leader of the Nationals, had come to Tamworth and won Windsor's old seat of New England.

It was a symbolic act of a party reasserting control over a region they had been run out of by an upstart like Tony Windsor. Ever since, there had been a rivalry between the stray and the herd, and especially between Windsor and Joyce, a man who lived his life as a walking stereotype, an embodiment of the way city folk see country people.

Windsor wasn't about to let the challenge go unanswered. He lost his 2016 re-election bid, but then, that happens sometimes. He's a sucker for impossible fights, he says. There's nothing wrong with losing, if you do it with dignity.

* * *

Politics wasn't Tony Windsor's original career plan. By the time he hit twenty-seven he was a farmer with a degree in economics and an interest in agri-politics. He would turn up to meetings and listen to the discussions, but that was it, until a family friend stepped in and said if he really gave a damn about this stuff, the only way to make anything happen was to get involved.

Windsor's father had been killed in a farm accident when he was just a kid, and that family friend had served as a father figure. His word had weight, so when he said the Nationals were really the only game in town, Tony Windsor signed up.

'The world is run by those who turn up,' Windsor says today.

From the start, he had a way of making people mad. He was headstrong and honest, qualities that don't always resonate in the world of politics. No one likes a critic, especially a critic on your own side, and no one likes a rank amateur pointing out your flaws. Change, after all, is hard. Change is risky. And the people who lose most from change are those who benefit most from the status quo, the people who have been doing the same thing the same way for decades.

It was 1991 when Windsor first ran for preselection for the state seat in Tamworth. He talked about how the Nationals had lost their way, how the party didn't represent the people it claimed to. The party was taking the side of the bosses, Windsor said, when it should be representing all the people living in country areas.

That fight ended up a bitter one. Of all the candidates running for preselection, Windsor won seven of the nine biggest branches, but the delegates who were supposed to maintain the integrity of the system, at that time, were under no obligation to respect the outcome of the vote. Windsor was critical of them and their way of running the system, so when it came time to nominate a candidate, they seized on allegations that Windsor was a drunk driver, and it went to a guy who had won just one branch.

Once word got out that the party aristocracy had been messing around with the democratic process, the local peasantry started to revolt. Windsor was asked if he might like to run as an independent. He suggested they put a meeting together with a good cross-section of the community, and he'd see if they were interested. On the night, forty people turned up, including the founder of the wheat board and some disgruntled National Party people. They urged him to run, but Windsor said he had no money.

'I said if we do this, we do it to win, and to do it we need money,' he said.

The seat he was running to represent was held with a 70 per cent majority by the Nationals, and Election Day was just three weeks away. The crowd didn't care, and that night they handed over $8000 and a promise to raise more.

So, with three weeks to campaign, Windsor hit the road as an independent. Then about ten days out from Election Day they decided to test the waters by holding an official opening. If it worked, they knew they had a chance. If it didn't – well, that was too bad.

His campaign managers picked out a little hall in Tamworth for the party, thinking that no matter how many turned out it would look like he had packed out the room, but Windsor overruled them. Go big or bust was his thinking, so they booked out the Workman's Club, the biggest building in town, and that night 800 people turned up to hear what he had to say. That's when they knew they had a chance.

And when voting day came, they won by a landslide. A band of complete novices had overthrown a major party on home turf and catapulted Tony Windsor into a political career.

Windsor didn't go home that night. He left the after-party at three o'clock in the morning and stayed at a friend's place. Four hours later, at seven o'clock on the mark, the leader of the Nationals called the house looking to talk business. The count was progressing and it seemed more and more like it was going to be a hung parliament.

Overnight, Tony Windsor had become one of the most influential politicians in New South Wales state politics. His vote was one of four that would let former state Premier Nick Greiner form government, and when the ICAC ruled that Greiner had used the offer of an executive job to help secure the Liberal Party's position, Tony Windsor helped take him down.

Tony Windsor's career in state politics would last ten years before he decided to try his luck in Canberra. Windsor went federal for what he calls a 'fairly obscure' reason: competition policy. From the 1990s on, state and federal governments had been talking about the need to centralise, to consolidate and deliver efficiencies in the way services were provided. Bigger was always better, in this line of thinking. Bigger was more efficient. Economies of size and scale were the best way to deliver the greatest number of outcomes, for the greatest number of people.

So, as time went on, services started to be wound back from rural areas towards the cities. When a hospital or clinic got old and needed replacing, a nameless bureaucrat in a capital city somewhere decided it would be cheaper to move it to a bigger town an hour down the road. When the hospitals in those towns got old and needed replacing, it was cheaper to move them to a bigger population centre even further away, taking with them money and people and easy access to health care. Bigger was better, unless you happened to be little or remote.

'A lot of this has got to do with how Hanson's come out of the fire,' Windsor says.

* * *

The first thing you learn in politics, Windsor says, is that you can't trust anyone. The second lesson is that major party politicians are victims of their own ambition, or, at the very least, the ambition of their colleagues.

'The weakest position in politics is Cabinet,' he says. 'I had plenty of opportunities to become a minister and all this, but one of the weakest positions you can be in in parliament, is to be in Cabinet. We have this view that that's where it all happens.

'The last twenty years prove that's all bullshit.'

These days, insiders on both sides of politics point the finger at Tony Abbott for making Australian politics entirely unworkable, but really he just accelerated a process that had already been going on for a long time.

Over the past half-century Australians have been losing faith in their political class, a trend that is shown in the longest-running survey of Australian voters conducted by the ANU. At the most recent survey, 79 per cent of people did not watch the leaders' debate, yet 65 per cent said they cared a great deal about who won the election. The graph showing the number of people who had always voted for the same party resembles a stock-market crash and was down to its lowest point ever at 40 per cent, while the number of people who thought politicians had become self-interested and insular had ballooned. One in five said it didn't matter who they voted for. Half thought government was run to benefit a few narrow interests, while almost half said they were unhappy with democracy in Australia.

The breakdown of political parties and the move towards government by coalition is possibly the only reliable trend currently at work in Australian politics. At the 2016 election the number of votes for minor parties was higher than at any point since 1949, with the two major parties feeling the pain. The Coalition failed to win a significant majority government, while Labor won 15 seats in the House of

Representatives from second place thanks to the flow of preferences, the highest number in its history.

Tony Windsor was just one of the first to see it and then turn it to his advantage.

'The Prime Minister likes to think they're the boss – in a hung parliament, they're not,' he says. 'It took Gillard a while to work out that she was not actually the boss. She was the leader of a major party in a minority government. She did a very good job of that, but she wasn't the boss.'

And Tony Windsor was one of those who put her there. When the 2010 results didn't turn out as expected and the election was declared a draw, the country independents became kingmakers when it was left to them to sort it out. Bob Katter, Rob Oakeshott and Tony Windsor agreed to negotiate together, and so found themselves in a position to decide who would form government.

As far as Julia Gillard and Wayne Swan were concerned, they had no chance with the country MPs and decided that if they were going down, they might as well treat them with a little dignity. Tony Abbott read the situation the same way, though his approach to negotiations differed. He decided he was dealing with a bunch of country hicks who were prisoners of tradition and would naturally swing right. In the end, Gillard came to the negotiations expecting nothing, while Abbott expected them to kneel.

Tony Windsor had thought Tony Abbott was a jerk ever since John Howard was around. One time, while waiting his turn to speak in the House of Reps, Windsor remembered a shadow falling over him and Tony Abbott, then manager of government business, loomed large. Abbott said the government had urgent business to discuss and would the independents mind not speaking.

Windsor told him no. He'd been waiting while the Liberals and Labor went at each other for too long now and he was determined to speak. Abbott asked him whether he might be a good sport and consider keeping it short. Again, Windsor said no. Abbott stood over him then and told him there was an easy way to do this, or a hard way. The government could, if it wanted to, use its numbers on the floor of the House to gag him.

'And I said, "Well, let's do it the fucking hard way,"' Windsor says. 'And I went on and spoke for as long as I needed.

'After that he never bothered me. All bullies are weak. And all they need is to be confronted.'

So, when it came down to deciding who to support in forming government, Abbott let the days wind out. He had it in the bag, his thinking went, but it was only in the second week, his people suggested, that there were no guarantees and that he might want to start talking to the independents.

Fanatics and diehards fumed that the independents didn't immediately default to the Liberals, but then the independents owed no one their allegiance and were taking the decision seriously. Out of the next government, Windsor wanted infrastructure such as a decent NBN, he wanted better funding for schools, and he wanted action on climate change.

It was fellow independent Rob Oakeshott who designed the process for negotiating with the government, and the three independents worked together to present a united front. All sorts of meetings went on in that two-and-a-half-week period. A climate-change expert flew out from London to advise them on which party had the better policy. Treasury made time to go over the financial state of the economy and to help evaluate which party had the better economic agenda. They met with ministers and shadow ministers. They met with Gillard, and they met with Abbott.

'Towards the end of the second week, Tony [Abbott] was getting desperate,' Windsor says.

'He was leaving messages on my phone saying, "Listen, I'll do anything to get this job. I'll do anything. You tell us what you need." It became very obvious he was just in panic mode.'

That's when Abbott started trying to buy their support. He had a list of things he was going to give the independents, and he even offered Tasmanian MP Andrew Wilkie 'two Hobart hospitals when he only wanted one.'

'All of that said to us that this bloke wasn't serious about running the term of a hung parliament,' Windsor says. 'Bronwyn Bishop said they would have gone back to the polls as soon as they were able to. All these promises and commitments were just made to get the job. It became very obvious that he was full of shit. He wasn't interested in real policy.'

It took sixteen days for the results of the election to be called, and on the seventeenth Windsor and Oakeshott threw their support behind Julia Gillard's government while Katter went with Abbott. While the left gloated over the shock win, the commentariat and Abbott's warriors on the right fumed. Blinded by their own hubris, they had been outmanoeuvred, and Abbott sought his revenge, spending the next three years punishing Gillard, and then Rudd, by opposing them on every single point, on every single issue.

Abbott's theme in the Gillard–Rudd days was that a Labor–Greens coalition would see the country grind to a halt. The 'unworkability' of a Labor government, or a

Labor–Greens coalition government, gave him a hard target against which to land a punch. Upon taking office in 2013, Abbott's target shifted to the Senate crossbench, which left him swinging at smoke. Every time the Senate refused Abbott and sent back another of his bills, he used it as another example of how the system was broken and how it needed fixing, particularly in his favour.

Which is one way of looking at it. The other is to recognise that power is a cooperative relationship and no independent owes fealty to a party. The only people who matter to them are their constituents, and if a government has a mandate to govern, independent MPs and the Senate crossbench have a mandate to resist anything they feel might rewrite the social contract to disadvantage their people.

Not that this way of thinking is popular. Saying no doesn't make any friends, and rebels have a way of making frightened dullards uncomfortable. Instead, it's easier to tolerate them and repeat the idea that they may make life hard, but at least they're weak.

Tony Windsor's career proves otherwise. His lesson is that you don't need to be king to make a government remember people they might prefer to forget.

You just need to be in a position to decide who sits on the throne, or the limits of their reach.

Chapter 14

ENTRY LEVEL

IT'S COLD TODAY IN HEYFIELD, CENTRAL GIPPSLAND. THERE is a bitter chill on the wind and the drizzle is starting to come down. Over in the distance iron structures rust and a stray cat works its way through piles of timber.

The air smells like freshly cut wood and there's an inch-thick layer of sawdust beneath Ricky Muir's feet. It's getting close to five o'clock now and he has already apologised twice for fobbing me off, but he's got a client waiting on an order.

'Don't worry,' I say. 'I've got time.' He clears a spot over by the arm of a backhoe, which I lean up against and watch him work as he takes apart a log with precision using a Lucas Mill saw. Each time, he measures out a fresh plank of wood, adjusts the circular saw and then drags it back through the log. When he gets to the end, he rotates the diamond-tipped blade and pushes it back through the brown stringy gum. It glides through like butter, he says when he gets a moment,

taking off his ear-covers so he can hear me. Not like that
last log. That was a hard wood. It fought back.

Ricky used to be a federal senator. These days he's back
to civilian in hi-vis and now owns the sawmill where he used
to work in his time before politics. He runs it with his wife,
Kerrie-Anne, who works on site along with his oldest son.
She's studying a business course to help out with the operation
and is working her way up to that law degree she's always
wanted. Life is constantly interesting with Ricky, she says
in a quiet moment. Whatever he does, she's right there with
him. She never expected to end up in politics, and she never
expected to end up working in a sawmill.

The pair bought the place from the previous owner, who
was waiting on a double lung transplant. The old man had
been a smoker and was just waiting to die, Ricky reckons,
so taking care of the business got too much. A lot of the old
customers thought it had been abandoned, until the couple
came along with the money they had saved from politics and
offered to take it over.

Heyfield might seem like a place far removed from
politics, but get lost on the two-and-a-half-hour drive out
of Melbourne and you'll end up in Morwell, the heart of
the Latrobe Valley, a regional city of working-class people
whose name was made famous by the Hazelwood Power
Station. For decades, these were the people who kept the
lights on for Melbourne, until their power plant lived well
past its use-by date, and became too old and too dirty to
keep running. So the plant closed, and one in five people fell
out of work. Now they're hearing talk that the paper mill
might be closed down too.

If it happens, they'll be in trouble. Melbourne, that city
whose name gets printed in Helvetica on the side of tote

bags alongside New York and London and Paris, tries to avoid coming out to Gippsland whenever possible, and the people of Morwell know they're never going to see their town on a T-shirt. In the grand scheme of things, they don't matter all that much, a fact of life they have understood since 9 February 2014 when a bushfire lit up the coal pit outside Morwell that fed the power plant and grew into a fiery hellmouth that burned for forty-five days as it spewed toxic smoke over the town.

Depending on who you ask, the feeling is that regional Victoria has been in decline as of late. Melbourne might be making a fortune buying and selling real estate, but unemployment is still high in Gippsland. Melbourne is the economy of Victoria these days. Cut it from the social fabric of the state and the whole place would probably be in recession.

But that's politics. Here, in Ricky's sawmill, he thought he could escape that world for a time and honestly didn't think people would remember him. Before long, he thought, he'd just go down as a footnote in some dusty history book and that would be that.

He was wrong. His time in the Senate might have been due to luck, and it might have been short, but it also made him an advocate for his community. These days every time he posts a stray comment on Facebook his phone once again lights up with reporters looking for more.

Then there are those trying to get him back into the game. They come into the yard as customers, or pretending to be customers. They sidle up to the front desk in the office and with one arm on the counter they start up a conversation that eventually turns its way to politics.

Once this whole region was a stronghold for the Nationals, Ricky says, but now the rank and file are starting to lose faith. They're angry and confused. They're looking for an alternative, someone who will give it to the bastards – and that's where Ricky fits in, they say.

Why doesn't he join up with One Nation?

* * *

Tonight's the night the kids play footy. It's icy outside, but that's okay because their club has a hall, and there are sausages on the barbecue. There was a party over the weekend and the beer-can rings on the floor say it was a big one. We pull up chairs at the only table standing and crack two beers of our own. Kerrie is there, and so are the kids, and then we start to talk about politics while they're running around chatting and playing on phones.

Walking into the Senate Chamber the first time was breathtaking, Muir remembers. He was a complete novice then, an outsider in the political world and entirely out of his depth. Prior to being elected, Ricky Muir's only experience with politics had been watching his father and grandfather swear at the television. Going in, he thought the system was rigged. He didn't know anything about it, or how it worked, and he didn't need to. Either way, one of the major parties won and the government was run by people who had no idea what the rest of the world was like.

To this day, he says there was no way he could have prepared for what awaited. No amount of reading or training could have made him ready for political life. It was something you had to learn by doing.

And if Ricky Muir had no love for politics going in, politics also had no love for him. From the moment he walked in the door, it decided he shouldn't be there and did everything it could to get him out. Here was a guy who had never worked as a staffer, who was poor, white and working class, a 'car bogan' with little education and no idea about politics or the office he was about to take over. For a time, there was even a video floating around of him throwing kangaroo dung at family on a camping trip. From the public there was a frustration, which was shared in private by some career politicians, about how a guy like Ricky Muir could be let loose in the Senate. It was a sentiment backed up by thinkpieces and venomous commentary that were so downright hurtful Monash University's Nick Economou once called Muir the most hated politician since Pauline Hanson.

'That was the first attitude in the media,' Muir says, thinking back. 'He doesn't belong here. He doesn't have the education. He hasn't been a staffer.'

But, Muir says, he knew he was green the first time he walked into the Senate Chamber. Everything was red, prim and proper. Everything was big. Processes were established, and followed, always and to the letter. It was like nothing he had ever seen, and nowhere he had ever been. It was official, it was legal, it had authority.

And it wasn't long before everyone saw the rookie, smelled vulnerability and moved to exploit it.

Almost immediately, his party had agreed to a deal with Clive Palmer's party to work together where 'practical'. At the time, everyone was trying to work out what the composition of the Senate was going to mean for the future of the country and as soon as ink was put to paper, people were doing the maths to guess at how things might play out.

Suddenly, there was huge interest in Ricky Muir: who he was and what he was about. Everyone wanted to know his story, including Mike Willesee, who asked for an interview. Interviews were what parliamentarians did, Muir thought, so he agreed to do it.

As far as media interviews go, it was a deafening bastard of a screw-up.

'I was absolutely petrified,' he says. 'I was in this tiny little room, big cameras, big lights, Mike Willesee in front of me. I wouldn't have been able to remember my own name if you asked me.'

The night they were to tape the thing, Muir was overseas for the first time in his life. He was away from his family, and from Kerrie, his wife and strongest supporter. The camera gazed unblinkingly through every stutter, through every awkward pause. It took everything down and didn't miss a second. When he stopped to take a break, it kept watching, and the night it went to air, Willesee put it all on the record.

Ricky Muir had been waiting for it. He knew they had bad footage. He hoped they wouldn't use it, but of course they did, and when it went live, he didn't even watch at first. He just laughed. It was his first lesson in politics: the system is more afraid of what you represent than you are of it.

As far as screw-ups go, it was a disaster. He had been pantsed in front of the entire country. He was a loser in a world in which the only people who mattered were winners. Any professional with a major-party affiliation would have slumped onto the backbench for the rest of their very short career, but Muir was different. For him, the pressure was off, and now the national press thought they had taken his measure, everybody left him alone, giving him a chance to regroup.

It was a chance he took with both hands in the lead-up to his first speech.

He had written the thing himself, though to this day some refuse to believe it. None had read the whole thing in its entirety, either. Muir had asked a few people what they thought about different parts, but never gave away the game, and on the day he read it, it immediately went national. Video of it circled on social media. The whole country watched. He had never owned a suit, he said, and had no intention of owning one – that is, until the day he was elected. He was working class, a country kid who grew up below the poverty line and who had always wanted to work with his hands. Now he was here, he put on the uniform of the political class out of respect to the office, but he promised it wouldn't change him.

It was a sparkling, textbook Cinderella story about an ordinary guy who lucked out by landing a powerful position. He had taken time to scrub up, school up, only to come back more together than he had ever been.

'Everything changed from that point,' he says.

It wasn't all golden, though. In the time he took to regroup, there were problems in his office. Operating as an independent, or a representative of a minor party, makes a person vulnerable to any political operator with a little bit of hustle and a compelling pitch. Without the talent pool of the major parties to draw on, lone operators have to judge for themselves who they want to hire. Get it wrong, and everything can quickly get out of hand.

Less than two months after the 2013 election, the Victorian branch of the Australian Motoring Enthusiast Party split from Muir, and then the problems in his office started. For a time, his was a house divided. Not knowing anything about politics, and afraid to speak to anyone, he had hired veteran political operator Glenn Druery as chief of staff, on the advice of his party. Muir sat in the chair with Druery as regent who ran much of the operation in those early days. Druery controlled the diary and shadowed Muir to every meeting. In one story that ran in The Conversation, it was Druery who spoke, not Muir.

'We are not here to have a fight,' Druery told journalist Michelle Grattan, and in doing so signalled the government on the need to deal.

'Help Ricky achieve some good things from time to time – some things he's interested in – and I believe a good working relationship can be established.

'You are there to do things. Some people call it horsetrading. I prefer to call it getting along.'

Druery would get the sack, however, after he fell out with Keith Littler, the founder of the Australian Motoring Enthusiast Party, and the preference whisperer was escorted from the building by security. Susan Bloodworth, who ran Muir's electorate office back in Victoria, reportedly quit in protest. Six days later, Peter Breen, former New South Wales state politician and a lawyer with a certain affection for defamation law, would also get the sack. Druery's replacement, Sarah Mennie, later resigned too.

Druery did not go quietly, and was soon giving interviews, talking about a bizarre alleged conspiracy called 'Plan Z', involving a plot by Keith Littler to take over the Victorian branch of the Australian Motoring Enthusiast Party and take Muir's seat. Druery said he had been a victim of the plot, and his first mistake was not watching his back. According to Druery, Peter Breen had been sacked as part of the same power play, though Breen insisted he had been sacked for taking a sick day and leaking an incident report concerning Keith Littler's bad behaviour to the media (an allegation he denied). How the report ended up in the media Breen didn't know, but he made sure to say he had shown it to Druery in draft form.

Whatever happened, on the way out the door, Druery made it clear that there was no way Ricky Muir could survive without him.

'Ricky's a good guy,' Druery told Crikey in August 2014, 'but he is very inexperienced, and he left school early.'

Littler, for his part, declined to comment, but in 2015 he and his wife resigned from Senator Muir's office and moved back to Queensland.

Meanwhile, Druery landed on his feet, eventually helping elect Derryn Hinch and securing a job as chief of staff in his office. Sarah Mennie would join him in Hinch's office, but would later end up with Robbie Katter. Peter Breen, meanwhile, washed up with One Nation, doing a tour in Senator Brian Burston's office.

* * *

To this day, people still like to tell Ricky Muir he had no right to be in politics, that he was an outsider with no experience. He had earned just 0.51 per cent of the primary vote, in an election that saw one-third of the Senate vote going to neither of the major parties.

That's when he tells them that if people weren't voting for independents in the first place, he wouldn't have been elected.

'This was already happening well before I came on the scene,' he says. 'People were already looking for someone outside of the major parties.'

The Australian Motoring Enthusiast Party might have had few policies outside their immediate area of interest, but on all other things they said they would operate on a case-by-case basis. To party hacks and policy wonks the idea was insane. To commentators and observers, not being able to predict the result from a predefined ideology was frustrating. On any issue outside cars, there was no telling what he might do.

Maybe it was crazy according to conventional wisdom, but it was also liberating. Muir couldn't believe how politicians from the major parties would come up to him and whisper in his ear that he was doing the right thing on a particular issue, making the right choice during a certain vote, only to vote with their party against him when it came down to the crunch. Every time.

It was something that to this day Ricky Muir can't understand. He could accept that horsetrading was a part of politics. Without it, an independent couldn't get anything done. But he was an ordinary guy who grew up in an environment in which you lived by your word, and now he had to get by in an environment in which professional politicians were measured more by the successful use of power than what they actually delivered.

Ricky Muir's value was his ordinariness. It was a quality that allowed him to measure both sides of a debate against what he knew the implications would be for people like him. He was walking, breathing proof-of-concept for the idea that seventy-six random people picked up off the street and thrown into the Senate would be so terrified of screwing up, they would actually take their job seriously.

It also meant that during his time in office, Tony Abbott, the Oxford-educated career politician and born-again man-of-the-people, ended up having to deal with an actual man of the people, and Abbott didn't like the outcomes. Muir was too unpredictable, the line went. He could make an agreement one morning and then a few hours later back out.

Not that the government made it easy. Eric Abetz, the Liberal Party powerbroker from Tasmania, was the point man for Abbott's negotiations with the Senate crossbench, and he was hopeless at it. Abetz had all the charisma of an ancient vampire, recently risen and looking to feed. Then there was the complete arrogance of a government that considered the Senate more a formality than a mechanism for checking its work. One night a 700-page piece of legislation appeared in Muir's inbox at ten o'clock with a note attached saying the government wanted to vote on it in the morning. As far as Muir and the other senators were concerned, it wasn't going to happen.

Tony Abbott used the threat of a double-dissolution election to clean out the lot as a means of keeping the Senate crossbench in line, but it was Malcolm Turnbull, the self-made multi-millionaire, who actually rewrote the rule book to try to make sure people like Ricky Muir could never be elected again. The voting system Turnbull introduced, with support from the Greens and Nick Xenophon, ensured minor parties and independents would need a significant primary vote in order to make it over the line. The idea was to purge with a double dissolution and get back to business as usual. Only professional, career politicians with money to run a grey, lifeless campaign would be allowed to debate public issues.

'You know, I went in thinking that the system was skewed to suit the major parties' needs before I got elected and then they used my name to skew the system to suit the parties' needs,' Ricky says.

He had known that it was coming for a while. The media might have warmed to him, and the public who followed politics respected him, but the idea that he, and others like him, didn't belong still had currency among political people.

The first sign came when the government stopped talking to the Senate crossbench. Instead of negotiating to find themselves a double-dissolution trigger, they found it in the form of the Australian Building and Construction Commission legislation.

When the people of Australia learned they would go to an election in 2016, it was a freezing night in the Briagolong pub and the Muirs were sitting in the beer garden. It was Kerrie's birthday, and Mother's Day, but their celebrations were cut short by the announcement. There was no TV in the pub, so Kerrie kept trying to stream it on her iPad as its connectivity dropped in and out.

It would be an election campaign he was all but guaranteed to lose. Ricky had no money for the fight, but he had spirit.

Spirit, though, was not enough, and he would lose, replaced by Derryn Hinch, the 'human headline', former radio shock-jock. Like Muir, Hinch had to climb up the learning curve and would quickly find out that a good job in radio had more political reach than a job as a politician. In radio, he was a god of the microphone who threw lightning across the airwaves against child abusers, flip-flopping politicians and backroom dealers. In politics, he was fresh meat in the lion's den, a place he had until then only known from the outside, and was just another vote among seventy-six.

* * *

When people ask him to run as a One Nation candidate, Ricky Muir asks them why they think he should. They usually start out the same way, saying they don't support all One Nation's policies, but what they want is someone who is going to raise hell.

'Interestingly, they think that her policies on immigration are aggressive, but they want someone to, as the Democrats might say, keep the bastards honest,' he says. 'And they want a growing force, not just a single representative, but something a little bit stronger to spook them into line, I suppose.'

It's no surprise to him that people are turning to One Nation. The Libs never gave a damn about ordinary people, while Labor have given up their blue-collar roots. It's one of the reasons he turned Labor down when they came calling to see if he would run for them, and why he tells those who say he should run for One Nation that it's not going to happen. That said, in June 2017 Muir signed on with the Shooters, Fishers and Farmers Party, the same people who narrowly won in the New South Wales Orange by-election after a 31.6 per cent swing against the Nationals.

'Politics is very much out of touch,' he says. 'Very, very, very much. And that's the rise of One Nation. Everybody just having enough, of having elected representatives getting in saying, I'm going to do this for their electorate, that for the electorate, and once they're elected, having the party tell them exactly what to do. Or just falling for the typical tit-for-tat politics.

'Pauline Hanson is going to grow, I don't think she's going away at the next election.'

Chapter 15

A LONG TIME BETWEEN DRINKS

AT THE END OF A LONG SITTING WEEK, AFTER FLYING BACK from Canberra, John Madigan used to take half an hour to sit in St Patrick's Cathedral along the main drag in Ballarat to help take the edge off. It was his way of dealing with the liars and the cheats and the crooks in politics.

Madigan is a teetotaller and isn't hungry, so he doesn't order when he walks into the Golden City Hotel across the road from St Pat's. Under his AEMP work coat is a thick flannel shirt with sleeves stained with grease. When he shakes hands, it's like a vice.

'Five years,' Madigan says. 'That's ten per cent of my lifetime. Five years in Canberra, went like …'

He clicks his fingers.

'If I never went into parliament again, I had a crack. I tried my hardest to help people.'

These days, Madigan's back to being a blacksmith. He doesn't miss Senate life, he says, and never let his ambition fool him into thinking it was more than it was.

'People can easily become seduced,' he says. 'But life goes on. The country, the nation goes on in spite of Canberra, not because of it.'

He was never supposed to be in politics in the first place. He was a tradesman who had only run as a placeholder candidate for the Democratic Labour Party in 2010, which had not won a seat in over three decades and didn't expect to win one in that election. Then they did.

In office, Madigan operated with a motley collection of views. He supported the rights of refugees, but was suspicious of wind farms. He didn't believe in man-made climate change and had invited Lord Monckton, a climate-change sceptic, to speak in Australia. He was pro-life in the abortion debate and stood by Cardinal Pell, despite all the allegations against him. When things turned sour with the party in 2014, he left it and went on as an independent.

That was the side-show in the political career of John Madigan. The main event was always manufacturing, something that led to a working partnership with Nick Xenophon. The pair didn't always agree on the social issues, but both believed Australia had lost its ability to process the raw resources it was digging up, and that was bad news. Manufacturing offered meaningful work and good quality of life, but Australia had traded it in. Now it was a retail society, hawking back and forth an ever-expanding catalogue of poorly made junk.

Form triumphed over substance.

Madigan outlived the Gillard government and was around when Joe Hockey dared Holden to leave and took down what was left of the Australian car industry. Car making was the crown of manufacturing, a complex process of making 30 000 different bits and pieces that came together at just the right time to roar to life and drive off a production line. Now it was going, he and Nick Xenophon wanted the government to step in to keep regional economies across South Australia and Victoria from hollowing out, and so head off the spectre of rapid de-industrialisation.

But when they approached the government to talk about it, it was a conversation between two entirely different cultures. Madigan was a man from a different time, a guy who had earned his apprenticeship with Victorian Railways, when zero unemployment was the primary goal of policy. As an economic regime, it worked well, so well it solved the problems that provided the reason for its existence, and created new ones. All the excess machinery and idle labour left over after World War II had been put to work. For those with no money, it was paradise. For those with money, the business community, the rising inflation and stagnant growth it created were painful.

Across the world, the old order was swept away with Reagan and Thatcher and, in Australia, Paul Keating, whose gentle neoliberalism moderated the worst excesses of his counterparts elsewhere. After that, everything slowly became a commodity and the primary goal of policy was to keep inflation low. Successive governments chiselled away at Keating's checks and balances, though not completely. The result was that even in Australia, by the end of the first decade of the new millennium credit had become cheap and the easy money flowed. Efficiency was the word in a world of layoffs and restructuring, and those like Madigan just plain didn't fit anymore. When he spoke, it was in a language the rest of politics might tolerate but could no longer understand. Business management had become the most valued qualification for public office, with all the esoteric, baseless assumptions about personal ability that went with it. In that way, the logic of the merchant classes became the logic of public life and someone like Madigan, a blacksmith, just didn't square in that kind of calculus.

'These days, they're on about "Nation Building",' Madigan says. 'But it's a pie chart, not people. It's figures in a book, not people.'

* * *

Pushing people like Madigan to the margins eventually gave way to Hanson. Through a quirk of history, she had stumbled onto the national stage and in a short period of time forged Hansonism, a crude and confused reaction to the Great Transition. Her ethno-nationalism was small government and yet protectionist, with a deeply authoritarian streak that liberally borrowed ideas from the left and from the right. Her supporters came from the old agrarian communities that were losing their significance over time, and the working poor caught up in the churn. At One Nation meetings in towns that didn't have ATMs, those in attendance would tentatively raise their hand to talk about the dreaded neoliberalism and the apocalypse it promised in a manner that would not have been out of place at a Greens Party gathering.

To anyone paying attention, it was totally weird. Still is. At the time, there was little on the landscape nationally, or globally, to help place Hanson, and when she vanished, most people were just happy that they no longer had to think about what it all meant.

Hanson never really went away, though, nor did her supporters. They were still there, they just didn't have an outlet, until she returned.

'Sitting back and looking at what's going on, she's very good at identifying, talking about what people are worried about, that doesn't get spoken about by the major parties. She's good at playing to their fears,' Madigan says about Hanson.

Some things, he notices, have changed.

'Supposedly, she's for the battlers, but she votes with the government on everything.'

It's something all the independents say about Hanson: if you vote with the government all the time, you might as well apply for membership.

I ask him why he thinks she's back and Madigan thinks political correctness has something to do with it. Politics more than ever is becoming about exclusion and purity, he says. Things are so charged, so politicised, anyone saying something different becomes a target.

'When you just denigrate, vilify people, you know, you don't address their concerns. The fire keeps burning,' he says.

Pauline Hanson has been elected and she represents a constituency, rightly or wrongly. Even though he's out of politics, there's a sense he still feels caught in the same dilemma as everyone else: go hard, and you make her the underdog.

Malcolm Turnbull stumbled into that trap during the 2016 election when he said Pauline Hanson 'was not a welcome presence'. As soon as his words found ink, the metrics on Hanson's social media went through the roof and the phones wouldn't stop ringing.

It's why Madigan won't call Hanson a racist, though she tests him. I ask if he has seen the story today about the

One Nation candidate for the Queensland state election who stepped down after it came out he had threatened to kill Mihalis Kalaitzidis, a 25-year-old employee at his security firm.

Madigan hasn't, so I pass him my phone to show him the news alert. At the top of the page is an image of the man, an ex-cop, standing in his backyard giving a Nazi salute over a swastika mown into his lawn.

Madigan reads the top three paragraphs and gives it back. It's clearly painful for him. He looks away for a moment, before going on, talking about how some parties are in such a rush to contest an election and get some traction, they don't vet candidates. They just run them for the sake of running them.

But on the way out of the door, he says something else.

'My grandfather was Jewish,' Madigan says, fixing his eyes on me. On his mother's side. He says his family lived and worked in a Jewish neighbourhood. They were friends and customers. Good people.

Then he tells another story.

'See the Indian takeaway over there?' pointing across the way. 'The man who owns it has a wife and a young son. He works his arse off for them.

'He got out of his car one night back that way.'

He points off in the direction as he says it.

'Then these two ratbags came up behind him and beat the shit out of him, yelling things at him, right in front of his wife and son. His face was all swollen and bruised.

'He came into our office as a constituent. We helped him.

'If I had caught the bastards ...'

He doesn't finish the thought.

Me: There's talk of an election coming up.
Who are you voting for?

Him: You know, I reckon we should bring back a
little bit of Pauline.

Me: You serious?

Him: Yeah.

Me: Come on. You can't seriously believe half of
what she says.

Him: No, but she stirs the pot. She makes
them sweat.

**Conversation in the street, off Wilkins Road, Elizabeth Downs,
South Australia, 24 July 2015**

Chapter 16

FEELING THE BURNIE

It was 8.12 in the morning for the 8.30 flight to Burnie-Wynyard airport on the northwest coast of Tasmania, and the TV on the wall was recapping Trump's successes with a highlight reel of disappointment, fear and failure.

Trump had reached his first 100 days in office, an unofficial landmark for any new presidency. In that time he had bombed Syria and dropped the Mother of All Bombs on a cave network in Afghanistan. He started sabre-rattling at North Korea. He had tried to, and then failed to, set up a discriminatory Muslim ban for travellers heading to the United States, which shut down airports in the confusion. He issued a presidential decree to get started on building his wall. He was talking about slashing funding for most government agencies, and had put a freeze on any new federal hires, meaning the executive branch couldn't fill the lower and mid-level positions it needed. His whole administration was operating on a skeleton crew with only a fraction of the few thousand people needed to run things, and only twenty of the 550 political appointees requiring Senate approval had actually been approved. On top of all that, his campaign team was being investigated by the FBI and Congress for possible collusion with Russia.

It was, as *Foreign Policy* columnist Rosa Brooks had written, looking like Donald Trump was America's experiment with having no government. Trump had no policy and no idea. It is one thing to say you want to do something, but it is wholly another thing to attempt it and then to carry it through.

All Trump had, in the end, was fire and brimstone, and a fistful of missiles.

There were maybe fifty people waiting at the airport gate, and those who couldn't see turned around in their seats to watch the montage. Some, like the man with two young kids sitting across from me, refused to watch.

An expert in a pinstripe suit and *Wolf of Wall Street* tie flashed on the screen and told the presenters that Trump may be unpopular, but he hasn't lost any support.

'The business community still love Trump. We, the people who created jobs, love Donald Trump, and if you give us a chance to create millions of jobs, people are going to like him too.'

This was a sales pitch for a guy who was sinking, one of the most unpopular presidents in US history, one who admitted to the media that he never thought being president would be this hard and that he missed his old life.

'Just give us a chance,' the man in the tie said.

A big, cheesy grin spread across his face.

* * *

The plane was pointed in the direction of Tasmania, the tiny island state that was once the turf of Brian Harradine, a plucky anti-communist, strict Catholic chosen by the people of Tasmania to represent them for three decades. Harradine ended up with the balance of power in the Senate and used it to extract every cent he could from the government of the day.

Some people might call that extortion. Those people probably aren't Tasmanian.

There's a reason Harradine's successor, Senator Jacqui Lambie, has 'PUTTING TASMANIA FIRST' written in all-caps and splashed across anything bearing her name. Tasmania has an almost religious devotion to the idea of 'buy local'. On the mainland it might be good enough to buy Australian, but on the island, it's 'Buy Tasmanian'. There are ads on the television about it between the news reports on the ice crisis and the struggles of the northwest.

These were some of the things I had hoped to talk about with the senator, but she never agreed to my interview request, and her office never really explained why, just that it wasn't going to happen. Maybe, I thought, they didn't have time, or maybe it had something to do with how Lambie had been forced to sack her chief of staff, Rob Messenger, the guy behind much of her anti-Islam rhetoric, and just didn't want me sniffing around.

Which was fine, I thought. If Jacqui Lambie wouldn't talk to me, maybe her people would. After all, this is a woman who some, even some Tasmanians, still call Pauline Hanson's little sister. Both have strong things to say about Islam. Both wear their patriotism like they are wrapped in an

Australian flag. Both are furious women. Neither is a book learner. And, at least according to the data, disadvantage defines both Pauline Hanson and Jacqui Lambie voters. Though it's true that, on the whole, the further down the wealth divide a voter falls the more likely they are to vote for Labor or the Greens, put a voting booth in a poor neighbourhood in northwest Tasmania, where 14.31 per cent of the vote went to the Jacqui Lambie Network, or Queensland's heartland, and chances are those living around it will vote for Hanson and Lambie in numbers.

When *The Guardian* asked Senator Lambie what she thought about being called Pauline Hanson–lite in a profile published in 2016, Lambie rejected it outright. She had her own voice, she said, end of story.

It takes all of five minutes walking around Burnie to work out why that comparison would be offensive to Lambie. Pauline Hanson was a small-business owner who grew up in a political culture where Joh Bjelke-Petersen set the tone by running the whole state of Queensland like his personal fiefdom.

If Hanson knew business, Lambie knew welfare. Her story is the story of the region and Burnie, in its own way. She came into the world near Ulverstone and grew up in a broken family on the outskirts of Devonport, the next big population centre to the east. She was a high-school dropout who was pregnant by eighteen and joined the army when some friends agreed they would all go together, only once she put her name to the paperwork her friends ran.

Neither the army nor Lambie knew she was a few weeks pregnant at the time, and Lambie says that the army tried to kick her out when they found out. In the end, she spent a decade driving trucks and working in the military police, until a training exercise in 1997 had her carry a 40-kilo pack over a two-day, 40-kilometre trek through an obstacle course and field training. The Monday after, she woke up with a back injury that led to her discharge in 2000.

After that came a few long, hard years of struggle with bureaucrats and medical people and money. Eventually she got hooked on painkillers. The army didn't like it and cut her pension after they decided she was a screw-up and a fraud, based on footage taken by the private investigator they had sent after her, leaving her to raise two kids on the Disability Support Pension. She had no money to register her car, in those days, but she drove it anyway. When the fridge broke down, she lived out of an esky for three weeks.

Then just before Burnie began to sink, Jacqui Lambie tried to end it all. It was 14 August 2009. She'd been drinking that night and was out with friends when she decided that was it. She walked out the door, and in front of a car.

* * *

Dave's Noodles is one of the few places in town you'll regularly see anyone with skin a shade darker than pearl white. It's a cheap Chinese takeaway on the main drag with a handwritten sign on the front door saying that because of the prawn shortage there won't be any on the menu for a while and sorry for the inconvenience. It's the kind of place where the guy behind the counter takes two seconds to size you up as you walk in the door and defaults to handing you a plastic fork wrapped in a napkin with your order, even as you reach for the chopsticks. It's habit.

I've got a taste for noodles tonight and Dave's is looking good. There's a line, five people deep, and the place is halfway to capacity, though most people are getting their food to take away.

The novelty in a place like this is noodles in a box like you see on American sitcoms. I don't buy into it, so I get the Singapore noodles, have here, and I'm given a buzzer. I take a seat on a stall at the bench so I can look out through the window and onto the empty street.

Five minutes go by before I notice The Guy. I'm flicking through a local newspaper celebrating the decision to pump fresh money into the Queenstown mine when I see him. He's shoeless and in sweatpants and his belly is hanging out the bottom of his grey T-shirt. He's got to be about thirty and doesn't look homeless; just poor, or lazy, or maybe both. He's heading into the noodle shop and as my buzzer goes off he joins the queue.

I turn on my stool and see a woman sitting over at a table, back against the wall, gently supporting the hands of the toddler standing on her lap. She's got her pram within reach in case the kid plays up, and she's wearing tights, her hair pulled back in a ponytail, a puffer vest and thin, wire-framed glasses. Something about her speaks to money and comfort.

I see her focus on the guy as he walks through the door of the noodle shop and goes to stand in line. She scans him up and down and takes a moment to process. Then there's the look, that universal expression of unvarnished disgust.

Burnie is what you get when local authorities graft a service economy onto a dead or dying manufacturing base with moderate success. In a manufacturing economy, no one cares about where you are from, or what you look like, so long as you turn up for work on time, preferably sober, and do the job. It's hard work, but in return you get paid well enough, and eventually you might just put away enough to move up in the world, to become significant.

A service economy doesn't work like that. A service economy exists to help ease the burden on people with too much money by taking some of it, or a lot of it, off their hands. The best in the business know it's a smile-or-die kind of game where presentation is everything. Those who aren't built for that sort of world haven't got a chance and instead tend to just let go, with beer and drugs and video games. And it's here, at Dave's Noodles, where those two Burnies meet.

* * *

Green's is dead right now, but it'll rise again in a few hours.

The place is an institution in Burnie, a big little town of 20 000 people at the bottom of the world. It's a hole-in-the-wall dive that looks out over the massive port to the town's east, which brings in most of the money. There are photos of bygone regulars up on the wall and the beer here is cheap. Four bucks a glass, though the Eftpos machine is playing up again, Danni the bartender says, and yeah, it's quiet right now but when tonight really gets going, it'll be massive.

Bob sits on a stool in the corner so he can see the television. He's a big guy in jeans and a baseball cap wearing a hangdog look. Brock is the only other man in the place, standing over by the fire. He's on the phone, and when he gets off I buy him a Jim Beam and Coke.

It's his favourite, he says, and he's been drinking it ever since he learned to drink. He loves the taste. Brock is a little guy with fuzz on his chin, glasses and greying hair. He works at the nursery his parents own just outside town. His father built it from the ground up and he helps out to raise the seedlings and tend the plants, along with his sister's husband, a carpenter. Brock loves his sister to pieces, he says, and he even gave a speech at her wedding. There wasn't a dry eye in the house.

What's there to do in Burnie, I ask, throwing the question out to the room.

'Yeah, what is there to do in Burnie?' Brock replies.

'Burnie ain't what it used to be. That's for sure,' Bob answers.

Brock sips his drink.

'It ain't easy,' Bob adds.

'You know the paper mill used to employ seven hundred women to sort through the paper? That's gone now too.'

I ask if Brock has kids. He doesn't, he says; he thought he had once, but it turned out he thought wrong. He's thirty-seven and wants them some day. I tell him he's still got time.

Danni the bartender, though, has two: a five-year-old and a fourteen-year-old. She's tall and pretty, her dark hair tied back in a ponytail, and she's obviously bored out of her mind tending to the barflies, who call her a 'nice girl'. She grew up in Queenstown when it was still alive, before it was gutted three years ago when the mine closed. She doesn't have much to say about it. She moved to Burnie a long time ago, and she has her kids. Burnie is a beautiful place in the world, she says, and Brock agrees. Melbourne might be the big city, but it's a nice place to visit, not to live.

Her kids are no trouble, she tells me, though the eldest sometimes gives her attitude. They're not like some of the people who drift through Green's on a Saturday night, though. There'll be 150 people through the door tonight all looking to find oblivion at the bottom of a glass, and there'll be eight bouncers on to keep them in check.

Last night there was a fight, Brock explains. Two young guys took swings at each other. There was no harm done, just a couple of swollen faces and a torn shirt before the bouncers dragged them out. Happens all the time, really, but Brock tries to stay away from drama like that.

On politics, Brock says he met Jacqui Lambie once. He does odd jobs around the place and once bartended a function she had at the Butter Factory a block over. She's a good person, he reckons, not stuck up or anything like that, and she doesn't have time for stupid questions. Her sons play football, and they're really good blokes. He didn't vote for her, though, and isn't sure why. He's just not that big into politics.

Bob, though – now, he's got a story. Bob started work when he was ten years old as a newspaper delivery boy. The job began at five on a frosty morning, and Bob went on to spend a lifetime working for a wage. He did bits and pieces around the place in the construction industry until he retired, and now that he's pushing seventy, he thought he had earned the right to live for a while on the pension. Now he says the government have cut it right back.

'Bloody Liberal government,' he says.

There's your Lambie voter, though he doesn't say it. Push him far enough, he might even go for Hanson. Crushed by the right, abandoned by the left, and a guy starts asking, what's the point? Sure, she's a racist, and that might not exactly square with someone like Bob, but why not let the bull into the china shop? Watch the bastards squirm.

What's happened to him doesn't seem fair, I say. Bob doesn't say anything. He just drains what's left in his glass and makes a move to leave. As Bob pushes open the door, Brock leans over on his bar stool.

'I don't think Bob's doing so great,' Brock says.

Brock goes back to sipping his drink.

* * *

The day Trump announced his run for the presidency, Jacqui Lambie was overcome by a feeling of déjà vu. The first thing she did was walk over to the office of fellow independent and ex-PUP (Palmer United Party) senator Glenn Lazarus to ask if he had seen the news. He had. Both had the feeling they had seen it all before.

Clive Palmer, after all, used to be their boss and was supposed to be the man who would change Australian politics. A self-funded billionaire anti-politician with a genius for wedge politics and furious rhetoric, he branded himself as the bigshot who spoke for the little people and who couldn't be bought on account of his vast wealth.

Lambie didn't initially run on Clive's ticket, but had sold her house to run as an independent. Her only political experience was a brief membership in the Liberal Party where she stood for pre-selection in 2011, and some time spent working for Labor's Nick Sherry. This time around, as a stray, it didn't take long for her to realise that in politics, money is ammunition, and she didn't have the cash on hand she needed to shoot through.

So, she needed Clive – or, more exactly, she needed Clive's money, and on his ticket she rode into parliament with 6.6 per cent of the vote.

Not everyone in Palmer's party was happy about having her there. First among them was Alex Douglas, a man literally descended from political royalty. His great-grandfather was a premier of Queensland, his grandfather an MP and a distant relative was King Robert II of Scotland. As far as he was concerned, Lambie's people were a waste of time and space.

She came from 'Boganland', he wrote in an email that leaked soon after the election, 'a world we see daily and quietly hope will disappear'.

'The world is full of them demanding their right, in an odd way, to be heard.'

In two lines Douglas had looked into the future and written his own epitaph. When the Palmer United Party crashed and burned, it was Jacqui Lambie, not the blue-blooded political aristocrats, who walked out of the smouldering rubble.

* * *

Burnie today is a fortress of the fallen working class. The whole city is a beautiful stretch of beachfront real estate nestled between the hills dotted with villages that stretch back for kilometres. It is home to honest people, to whom family matters deeply, living against the shadow of industrial decline, substance abuse, boredom and a distrust of outsiders.

These are the two Burnies: one mild, the other strong. If Hobart is the political and cultural centre of the entire island, Burnie was its muscle.

These days, the old paper mill is a symbol for everything Burnie has been through in the good times, and the bad. To outsiders it was nothing more than a paper factory, but to the people who live in the region, it was an identity. The paper mill was where Dad met Mum, because that's where everybody worked. Sure, it may have stunk like sulphur from the chemical-pulping process, but to the people living here, it smelled like a decent home, food on the table and a university education for those with a little brains and a lot of ambition. The company even took care of its own, running a 'Hard Luck Fund' by matching any donations made by their employees. Even in the early 1990s, after the company abandoned its policy of welfare capitalism and brought in toe-cutting industrial relations professionals to help restructure the business, Burnie stayed loyal. The mill was theirs, and then one day it was gone.

And when the mill left, it became the metaphor for everything else happening to the region. The acid plant had gone, along with the paint and carpet factories, while the Caterpillar plant had been in decline. As if that wasn't enough, even the mine near Queenstown, which used to ship its dirt through Burnie's port, shut down.

All told, one in five people left the region. Today, the skies are clear, the ocean is clean, and while unemployment has slowly been ticking down, it's still aggressively high. All it takes is a bit of education for the young to up and leave for Hobart or Melbourne. Those who stay risk falling into unemployment, and one in ten people of working age between Burnie and Devonport don't have a job. That's a number that grows higher around some parts of Launceston too.

Burnie may not be an easy place to make a dollar these days, but it's an easy place to get by, and an easier place to die. Today there are two kinds of people who live in Burnie: outsiders who have retired, and locals who stayed. In one way or another, this makes Burnie God's waiting room, or maybe Satan's, depending on your attitude to authority and your taste in substances. The whole place has that laidback kind of vibe that makes it easy to let go, to ease into sweatpants and Ugg boots and low-wage jobs, doing what you can to get by. After that, you ease into middle age with two-point-five kids and dreams of a house on 'flat land'. You then ease into old age and late-morning coffees at Banjo's Cafe with the local newspaper, just like your parents might have done. The years bleed into each other until the day finally comes when you watch one last sunset over the ocean before you close your eyes forever. Then your friends and family ease you into the ground at the same cemetery where your mother and father and grandpas and grandmas were buried.

Burnie doesn't forget. Even today, the place calls itself the 'City of Makers', and over on the waterfront the town has built a museum to honour its golden years. Next to the industrial ruin of its paper mill, Burnie has built a Bunnings as a mausoleum.

Niche manufacturing, arts and crafts and cruise ships of retirees are the town's future now. In that way, it's like a hundred other towns throughout Australia. There's a boutique whisky distillery over the hills and a community of artisans making everything from cheese to fine Tasmanian wood kitchen tools. Every so often the town hosts a jazz concert or other arts event to raise the cultural tone of the community.

These new professions may not pay like the mill once did, but that's not going to stop Burnie from at least trying. The only thing the people here respect more than local pride is the ability to take a punch and get back up again. It's also what people tend to look for in their leaders. While Burnie leans towards Labor, it's these qualities that make Jacqui Lambie attractive to the people in Tasmania's northwest.

Or at least to one of the two Burnies. The other Burnie belongs to the people who like to laugh at her. They see her drive around in the Jacqui Lambie car, a roaring four-wheel drive with her name plastered all over it. She's a joke, they think. She's just too much. Too loud and too crass. She's good for a laugh, but that's about it.

It doesn't matter how high you rise in life, there will always be someone trying to put you in your place.

But then, those people are probably not from here, and they are outnumbered. People have had a gutful of politicians out this way, but Jacqui? No, she's different. She's a woman who speaks her mind and gives as good as she gets. She screws up from time to time, sure, but don't we all? And she's got time for everyone, you know. She's a local girl who has come up in the world, someone who put Burnie on the map in a big way. And if people don't like it – well, that's too damn bad.

* * *

It was Easter 2017 when another one of Pauline Hanson's videos appeared on the web. This time she was calling on the people of Australia to boycott Cadbury chocolate Easter eggs because they were halal certified. Buy Australian, apparently, has its limits.

Hanson's recommendation was that people should buy Lindt and Darrell Lea. Darrell Lea might have been an Australian company, but Lindt sure wasn't, and down in Claremont, Tasmania, where the Cadbury factory had gone through troubles, the reaction was Jacqui Lambie–style fury. The halal certification on their product meant their chocolate could be sent overseas, which in turn meant they could keep their people employed on an island where jobs growth was hard to come by. If Hanson wanted to send Australian jobs overseas, the locals weren't going to take it lying down.

So, the Australian Manufacturing Workers' Union (AMWU) came out swinging against a boycott. They, like other unions across the country, knew they had members who were One Nation supporters, but this seemed to be proof-positive for what union organisers across the country had been telling their members: Hanson didn't give a damn about working people.

Hanson had been trying to get a foothold in Tasmania for some time. One Nation's candidate, Kate McCulloch, barely missed out on a seat when she lost to the Greens candidate by 141 votes. Had Hanson concentrated her resources on Tasmania, instead of spreading them around other states, chances were the seat would have fallen to her.

McCulloch was a curious choice for One Nation. She was an outsider who first met Hanson in November 2007 when the One Nation leader made a run through the New South Wales semi-rural community of Camden. A year later McCulloch led the charge to keep a mosque from being built in the area and made headlines when the media called her the next Pauline Hanson.

When reporters called Hanson to ask what she thought, she hung up without saying a word.

The frosty reception didn't last, and a year after that incident McCulloch formally signed on to run as a One Nation New South Wales candidate, but it never went anywhere and she eventually washed up in Tasmania, where she once again put her hand up to serve as a lieutenant in One Nation's revival.

McCulloch, though, is still well respected among the nationalist, anti-Islam movement. She's got the right idea, her people say, and now the 2018 Tasmanian state election is rolling around, stuff is happening. On 29 March 2017, the Queensland One Nation branch formerly registered 'Pauline Hanson's One Nation – Tasmania' as a business name. A poll released by EMRS about this time surveyed 1000 voters and found growing support for One Nation, which was sitting on 5 per cent, with 9 per cent of respondents telling the pollsters that they would vote independent.

The only thing standing in their way is Jacqui Lambie.

Chapter 17

THE HOUSE THAT CLIVE BOUGHT

NICKEL IS A BUSINESS OF EXTREMES. WHEN IT'S GOOD, IT'S really good. When it's bad, it hurts. Nickel booms, and then it busts. That's how it goes. It's a lot like politics in that way.

The story of Queensland Nickel is one that goes back six decades to 1957 when a body of nickel laterite ore was discovered in central Queensland, about 175 kilometres west of Townsville. A joint venture was set up between US-owned Freeport Minerals Company and the Australian company Metals Exploration Ltd to dig it out of the ground.

Nickel was the ultimate get-rich-quick scheme. When prices were high, it was easy to make a fortune, but before you could turn dirt into money, you needed a refinery. So in 1974 they built a railway line out from Greenvale and opened a refinery at the end of its run in Yabulu, near Townsville.

The mine ran into financial trouble from the moment it started. Global nickel prices had tanked and the only reason it kept going was thanks to Joh Bjelke-Petersen, the Queensland strongman premier. Today the attitude in Queensland is that Uncle Joh might have been corrupt, he might have cut corners, but he made the state wealthy in the process.

Bjelke-Petersen's government had guaranteed the commercial debt to help the Greenvale mine stay viable, and when Alan Bond – the man who would eventually go down for fraud with A$1.8 billion owing in personal debts – bought the mine and took it over, nickel prices tanked, forcing the state government to shell out $100 million to keep it open. It was a band aid over a cancer, though, and when the mid-1980s rolled around there was no more nickel left in the ground.

When Bond went down, the Yabulu refinery was sold off, through a string of owners. The Greenvale mine closed in 1995 after giving up enough ore to produce 327 400 tonnes of nickel, and from 1995 the refinery was kept alive by sourcing nickel from places such as New Caledonia and the Philippines.

It was an oasis of stable employment for Townsville. Manufacturing might never have really been a part of Queensland's four-pillar economy, but the regular work offered by a processing facility in such an isolated place gave a lifeline to a town whose only other reliable employer was the military base.

Thing was, it was old. In 1997, BHP Billiton took it over with an idea to reinvent it. Their plan was to sink US$350 million into the plant to make it viable again by giving it greater capacity to process more ore. Problem was, management didn't listen to the workforce when they made the upgrade, and the result was a patchwork operation that was harder to maintain than the original plant built way back in the 1960s. With too many bottlenecks in the old plant, there was no way they could boost production to the 64 000 tonnes they needed to keep it viable, and when they were forced to shut their new nickel mine at Ravensthorpe, where costs had blown out to US$2.08 billion as of 2009, they put the refinery on the market.

Clive Palmer snapped it up for A$30 million, or 'beer money' as he called it at the time. It was a bargain, and in the transition BHP made sure the refinery remained in good repair, the spares shelves well stocked. They might have failed, but someone a little less ambitious could maybe find a way to make it work.

Palmer was not that man. He treated every aspect of his life as if he was Godzilla unleashed on Tokyo. He dreamed big and he talked big. It was these traits that had helped make him a Gold Coast property tycoon, and he was now about to put them to work in the nickel industry. This was the Clive who announced he would build the *Titanic II*, which never happened. He tried to build his own Jurassic Park with 160 animatronic dinosaurs, but intellectual property stopped him from using the name 'Jurassic Park', and the PGA golf tour, which had run tournaments for eleven years at the park, pulled out of the project entirely, leaving the whole thing a sad, absurd, unviable amusement park in the middle of nowhere.

There was also another side to Palmer, the part that liked to play the hero. When he swooped in to buy up Queensland Nickel, he talked himself up as the champion of the working men and women of Townsville. He showered them with gifts, luxury cars, overseas holidays, and for the first eighteen months things seemed to go fine. Among the workforce and the people of Townsville, there was real hope.

Pretty soon, though, the demands of running heavy industrial processes became more pressing. It wasn't possible to distract with gifts and promises. The grateful, feel-good vibe of the workforce began to wear thin as people looked to get down to business. The old management started to raise pressing issues about plant processes, but as they stood up to Palmer they were let go or pushed aside. Around that time, the new management brought in to replace them started to whittle down the workforce. Supervisors looked for reasons to fire people, chipping away at any worker or union manager who asked too many questions or pushed back.

With time, every dollar that could be extracted from Queensland Nickel was siphoned off and spent. BHP had set aside money for redundancy payments for the workforce, but Palmer spent it. Orders were no longer lodged and corners were cut on contract services. Management slashed budgets to the point where the maintenance crew were heading over to the scrap yard to scrounge parts. By the end, there weren't even spare nuts and bolts.

As it was happening, Palmer moved into politics, making him look a whole lot like an oligarch in the Russian sense. His pitch was that he was going to fix politics. He had more money than God, which meant he couldn't be bought, and he was going to repeal the mining tax, cut the carbon tax and raise a lot of hell in Canberra. The business was in trouble, he told the people who worked for him, and if he didn't do this, the plant would close.

To those who worked in his refinery, it seemed more like Palmer had got bored and was losing interest in them. He seemed to be trying to distance himself from the operation, handing official control over to his nephew, Clive Mensink.

Palmer saw the employees of Queensland Nickel as a ready source of conscripts. Daily emails updated them on the Palmer United Party and the screensavers on company computers were changed to support it. Those on a salary were expected to support the campaign run, while those on a wage were strongly encouraged to get involved. Among the workforce, there was a debate on how to react. Some genuinely believed the guy, while others figured that getting involved might earn them some goodwill when it came to layoffs. A tiny few, though, could see what was happening to the business and figured, correctly, that it was on borrowed time anyway, so nothing they did really mattered. Today they tell stories about the guys they knew over in processing who handed out how-to-vote cards for the PUP on voting day, expecting that they would be remembered when the time came. It didn't work out that way and once the election was over, they were swept away just like everyone else.

And on 15 January 2016, 237 workers were sacked from the Yabulu refinery. Three days later Queensland Nickel went into voluntary administration.

The Palmer United Party would last until April 2016, when it was formally deregistered.

* * *

What's happening to Townsville these days is a microcosm for the rest of the far north. Ever since the refinery closed, the place feels like a ghost town. It's got no water, thanks to a drought; electricity is expensive; crime is growing; and its population is falling. Anyone who can get out of town is leaving.

Even Samantha Larkins is getting out. Back when anger was raw and the hurt fresh, Sam became the unofficial voice of Queensland Nickel's workforce. Because Clive Palmer was involved, reporters brought their television cameras north and needed someone to lay it out for them, and Sam stepped up. She had been a union delegate with the AMWU who came from a 'very political' family on the Labor side of politics, so it was almost natural when people started to ask her to speak at rallies and answer reporters' questions.

'I described it as a small town that had just been ripped apart,' Samantha recalls. 'It was like a family and everyone was just thrown onto a garbage heap. People were just traumatised. It actually just traumatised a lot of people.

'And people still don't have all the facts. They haven't been able to sit down and work out the actual cost to the Townsville economy yet. Some people left. Some people managed to get FIFO jobs. The last accurate figure was that about three or four months ago about a third of the people still haven't got other jobs.'

It's hard to see a future in Townsville now, she says. It's why she took a job with a friend whose company extracts an essential oil from a native plant that grows in the Northern Territory. She didn't want to leave, she says, but she has no choice.

Steve Lovell, though, is staying put. He was thirty-seven when he started in a permanent job with Queensland Nickel, he says, and at the time he was trying to rebuild his life after he had lost everything in the 1998 Townsville floods. He thought he had a job for life with the refinery, working as a skilled tradesman on the maintenance crew, and he got a good few years out of it before Clive Palmer came through and gutted the place.

It's why Steve prefers not to talk about Palmer, whose income was pegged at $600 million by the BRW Rich List. Palmer might have added $50 million to his net worth since 2014, but at the time of writing Steve is fifty-six and on contract with a company servicing the rail network out that way, though with the end of the mining boom, they've said they're going to let him go for lack of work. For now he's doing as many hours as he can get, and when the contract wraps he'll do odd jobs until something comes up, or go to work for a labour-hire company and wait it out.

'Things aren't bright for my retirement, or for my children, or my grandchildren,' Steve says.

That said, he doesn't want to leave if he can help it. Townsville is home. It's where his family lives, including his five-year-old granddaughter. His future is Townsville's future and maybe, he says, if he can hold out long enough, the government might be able to get the Adani mine going and things will get better.

He's talking about the proposed A$16.5 billion Carmichael coal mine, which would spread out over 446 square kilometres, consume 12 billion litres of fresh water each year and produce 2.3 billion tonnes of coal over its 60-year lifespan. The Indian company behind the project has promised it will create over 10000 jobs during the construction phase of the project, with pre-construction work starting in October 2017 at the earliest.

So far the company has been running hard with that figure. During the 2015 Queensland state election it took out television adverts to promote it, though at the Queensland Land Court the company's expert witness Jerome Fahrer from ACIL Allen Consulting rejected the 10000 jobs figure and said the expected number would be fewer than 1500.

Other company representatives have also been talking about automating large parts of the process, potentially driving that number down further.

None of this even touches on the environmental impact of setting up a new mega-mine on the edge of the Great Barrier Reef, or the carbon emissions created by burning its coal.

For the most part, these concerns haven't moved Townsville, or coal country around the Mackay region. Australia was happy to take their coal when it needed cheap energy. People built their lives around it until one by one the old coal-fired power plants began to shut. The coal workers weren't needed anymore and were told they should find jobs in renewable energy. There are plans in the works for at least three new projects around Townsville at the moment, but they're not here, now.

If the choice is between an apocalypse now, or an apocalypse later, the answer comes in the form of a bumper sticker that reads: 'Don't take my coal job and I won't take your soy latte.'

I tell Steve it seems like he's being offered a pretty crappy choice, in all honesty, though he misunderstands me at first. He thinks I'm talking about the environmental impact. He's been reading about that lately, and especially what it might do to the reef. It's pretty bad, he says, but then I cut him off there to tell him he's got me wrong. Sure, the environmental impact is going to be huge, but there's another problem: coal's maybe got a hundred years' life. Tops.

'Seems to me that you've got a whole town of desperate people being offered a bum deal,' I say. 'I mean, however you feel about renewable energy it is getting cheaper all the time and it is a growth industry worldwide. Sooner or later, this mine's going to close and then your children, or your granddaughter, are going to have to deal with a great big hole in the ground and a town with no future. Again.'

Steve gets it. Personally, he'd love more renewable energy projects or something to happen with the port. He doesn't care what it is, but they need jobs right now and the only hero project anyone is talking about is the mine. At the very least, Adani will buy them time.

'Then we need government and their think tanks to ask what is going to be the next source of income,' Steve says. 'The smart money is when you can see the end of something and then think about how to create future prosperity.'

Maybe I'm cynical, I say, but that doesn't seem likely.

'You're right to be cynical,' he says, 'especially if you've seen what's happened so far.

'I don't know whether that is possible. I don't know whether I'll ever get another permanent job in the next ten or twelve years. I don't think we're capable of getting it together. We have so much in common but we seem to have more differences than things we see eye-to-eye on.'

It's why One Nation is doing so well in Queensland's far north, he says. As everything gets tighter and tougher, people are looking for something else. This is a trend reflected in the latest polls showing north Queensland swinging hard to One Nation, and in the way everyone has something to say about Pauline Hanson whenever they talk politics. The only thing holding a lot of people back is the nagging doubt that wonders whether they'll be able to actually get anything done at all.

Steve, though, thinks Pauline is another Clive, the guy who said he was going to do something and failed to do anything. Sure, Islamic terrorism worries him and he agreed with Theresa May when she said 'enough is enough' after the most recent terrorist attack in London. He even worries about immigration at a time when he sees the country struggling. None of that is going to decide his vote, though. All that matters to him right now are dollars and cents.

That's why Steve's going to park his vote with whichever party seems most likely to deliver – and for him, that's Labor. He likes how Queensland's Labor Premier Annastacia Palaszczuk has been fighting to make something happen for Townsville and he thinks Bill Shorten has the right idea at the federal level. Shorten has made a couple of trips out north now, and Steve thinks the Labor leader gets it.

Or, rather, he hopes.

'You can see that people are looking for something different because they know the democracy that we have at the moment is not working and especially here in Townsville, the divide between the rich and the middle, the working class is growing,' he says.

'We've seen this in the US with Donald Trump. Everyone being broke, year after year. And then to have it drop and everything's like a ghost town. If we're not careful, the same thing will happen here and you'll end up with people in power with some weird ideas that don't really help.'

Chapter 18

FLASHBACKS

RAHILA HAIDARY DIDN'T KNOW WHAT SHE WAS GETTING INTO that Sunday in November 2015. It was the twenty-second, and she was on her way to Perth's Parliament House to meet some friends. They were there to counter-protest, they told her, because up on the hill was a group of people who hated Islam and were holding a rally to show it. Someone needed to confront them, they said, and show them that hate wasn't welcome.

It was hot that day, about 35 degrees Celsius in the shade with no wind. The police were everywhere, down every street and around every corner with operational vans set up to monitor everything happening on this part of the landscape.

On her way to the counter-protest, Rahila looked up the hill towards the rally her friends had told her about. It was called Reclaim Australia and she knew they had been on television, but she didn't know much about them. Her friends told her they hated her religion, which confused her. Protesting a religion made about as much sense to Rahila Haidary as protesting the AFL. You might like football, or you might not. If you did, it was just another natural part of who you were and a common language that united you with everyone else who followed the sport. Sure, sometimes things might get heated, but you never took it out on the other side, because that made you a hooligan.

It was that kind of thinking that made her wonder about the protesters, who they were and why they hated her religion. Maybe, she thought, if she could just talk to them, she might find out.

* * *

About 200 people turned out for the Reclaim Australia rally that day, and I got there early to watch them all filter in. The whole thing had been set up on a small flat up the hill and Australian flags hung limply against a cloudless blue sky. After watching for a while, I took out my camera to shoot some photos. A woman who appeared Sri Lankan was standing nearby and asked me not to photograph her. Then someone from the other side of the tree-line called out.

'Oi,' came the cry. 'Put it away.'

The demand came from a tall guy in dark speed-dealer sunnies. He was wearing a blue singlet with the faint outline of Australia marked on his chest in white. He had rings on every finger, a persistent five o'clock shadow and was carrying a camera with a pricey-looking telephoto lens hanging off the end.

This was a public space in Australia. I needed nobody's permission to film or shoot photos and I wasn't about to ask. So, I stood my ground. I told the guy no and he looked down his viewfinder on his camera, pointed the lens in my direction and started to shoot photos of me. It was ridiculous. I pulled out my media ID and posed for the camera, until his interest was piqued and he came over to investigate.

I was about to learn that Reclaim Australia, as a group, recruit their own volunteer security to keep counter-protesters from infiltrating their ranks and causing trouble. If I wanted to hang around the rally, the man said, I had to be cleared before being allowed to shoot. He walked me over to the man in charge, a tall white man wearing hi-vis who was leaning over a table. He checked out my ID back to front and reluctantly decided to cut me loose.

After that the man in the blue singlet wanted to make friends. I pointed to his lens and said it was a nice piece of glass, explained I was a freelancer, and said I was there to cover the rally. Then I asked him what he was doing.

'Shooting photos. I'm independent media too, man, like you.'

The guy offered to introduce me to a few people and I told him to lead the way. The man he put me onto was Zayne Van Day. He had migrated from New Zealand and claimed to be an ex-paratrooper. He was a big guy, with red hair and a moustache. He was nice enough, in a lost sort of way.

'I do this because I want my daughter to grow up in a world that I did,' he said.

I asked what world that was.

'The eighties,' he said. This was Zayne's golden age, a time when neoliberalism was still new. A time where memories of the White Australia Policy were still fresh and minority groups still knew their place. A time when Rambo was a hero who slaughtered godless communists in numbers.

A time when men were men, geeks knew their place and women in bikinis were trophies to be won.

Then I made the mistake of using the term 'white man' in asking a question. Zayne found it offensive and said he preferred 'Caucasian'. This was identity politics inverted, severed from its context, and turned back on itself.

After that came a ten-minute lecture about the moral superiority of Christianity as a religion and Jesus's teachings, a feature of Reclaim Australia most commentators have failed to grasp, with the exception of comedian John Safran.

Australia, for the most part, gets ethno-nationalism. The country was founded on it when, in the same year as Federation, the White Australia Policy was codified. What it has never really understood is religion, and Reclaim Australia was as much an extremist religious movement as it was a movement concerned with restoring the status of the white man.

When he was done, Zayne said goodbye. He was on the bill to speak at the rally, he said, and he had to prep.

I wished him Godspeed, and was left to wander as the organisers set up the stage.

Circling back through the growing crowd, I found Bev Fussell, a tiny 78-year-old woman with white hair and an excited smile who was wearing the Australian flag. She was nervous about talking to me, she said, and immediately insisted she was not racist, though I never asked whether she was. She had never been to a political rally before in her life, nor had she ever been a member of a political party. This was her first time and so I asked what she was doing here.

'I'm not against immigration, we've had good people come into this country before. They didn't live on handouts,' Bev said.

'I'm here to stand for Australian values our forefathers fought for and to see that the Australian lifestyle, culture and laws that we have always known, carry on into the future. I'm not against Muslims, but I am against radical Islam and Sharia and halal.'

The country's first permanent mosque was built in 1861 at Marree, an outback crossroads town in South Australia's mid-north. I knew, because I had been there to see the replica that stands in its place. The men who built it had come from across South Asia to work as the country's first truckers, carting water and resources across huge tracts of landscape. In doing so they had opened up the centre of the country to British colonisation and development. These men of the desert were hard men, some Hindus, but mostly Muslims. They had been made to leave their families at home, to keep them from getting too comfortable in Australia, but those who managed to stay married into local Aboriginal and European families wherever they ended up. They were devout and prayed five times a day. They kept the Sharia. They ate halal and passed on the tradition to their children. Some of their descendants still abstain from bacon, though they no longer know why.

Almost half a century of immigration and integration resulted in exactly one case of violence. In 1915, during World War I, two men, Mullah Abdullah and Gool Badsha Mahomed, raised the Ottoman flag and attacked a train near Broken Hill. They gunned down four people and were in turn shot dead. What tends to get left out of this story is how the keeper of Broken Hill's mosque, and the community it serviced, refused to give them a Muslim burial. As far as they were concerned, they were Australians in a time of war and these men were murderers. They were traitors to their country and traitors to the faith.

I didn't say any of this to Bev then. Nor did I tell her about how there are more Buddhists in Australia than Muslims. Instead I asked how she had found out about the rally today.

'Facebook,' she said. Social media, that distributed network of blogs and chat groups operating across the internet, had carried Pauline Hanson's name and reputation as far afield as the United States, where even Pastor Thomas Robb, head of the Ku Klux Klan, knew her name. Social media was how these groups organised, how they recruited, how they framed and reframed the narrative to the point where an apolitical 78-year-old is so afraid of a small minority group that she winds up at a political rally draped in the Australian flag.

I asked Bev if she really believed the stuff these other people had been saying about Islam.

'You know, this morning I went onto Facebook and I quickly shut it down. I closed the thing. I couldn't watch it. It was a video of a stoning. We can't have that here.'

That's about when the United Patriots Front (UPF) turned up, led by blond-haired, blue-eyed Blair Cottrell, who had flown in from Melbourne with his lieutenants to yell down a microphone at the Perth Reclaim Australia rally. Among the loose constellation of extremist groups which made up Reclaim Australia, the UPF were the most militant. They were fascist, in the plainest sense of the word. By day, Cottrell and his lieutenants were a small band of tradesmen and council workers. They were there to announce a new political party, Fortitude, but the idea would go nowhere when the group struggled to get enough signatures together and couldn't find a candidate to run that didn't have a criminal record for anything from arson to sexual assault.

To a man, they were suckers who had bought into a fairytale that made a virtue out of strength and made them feel better about their lot in life. Their only real skill was a keen sense of theatre, which made them more like a crowd-funded boy band with a Hitler fascination than anything remotely resembling a serious political force.

When it came time for them to 'appear', Blair Cottrell stood at the head of a group of thirty or so men who gave a martial grunt that boomed out over the grass. Everyone turned to watch as they marched onto the field, waving the Australian and UPF flags like a military unit.

I asked Bev what she thought of these big, hulking, tattooed men, some hiding their identities beneath half-skull masks.

'I'm a little bit unsure of them,' she said. 'I've seen a lot of their comments on their Facebook, and there's harsh language and all sorts.'

But, she said, she didn't feel threatened by their presence. She didn't think they were trying to hijack her movement, either. Everyone was welcome, she said. Reclaim Australia was all about free speech, a line I had been hearing all day.

And then the speeches started.

* * *

It is no coincidence that Pauline Hanson arrived in Parliament at a time when anti-Islam protest group Reclaim Australia was making national headlines. Anti-Islam sentiment swept through Europe and parts of the United States, Reclaim Australia was taking up the cause Down Under. Along with Liberal National Party member George Christensen, Hanson was one of many high-profile figures happy to lean in, appearing before the crowds who had come together to stop their country being 'taken over' by Islam.

The first time was mid 2015. The same weekend that mounted police in Melbourne charged counter-protesters on horseback, Hanson stood to give a speech to a Reclaim Australia rally in Rockhampton, Queensland. She opened by telling the crowd who had gathered that she was not a racist, and Reclaim Australia was not a racist movement. They were patriots who cared deeply about their country, and that was it.

'We are a nation of many different cultures, actually one of the largest in the world, of about 176 different cultural backgrounds, which has made Australia what it is today. I want to explain to you my concerns about multiculturalism,' she told the crowd. The rest was the same speech she always gave: a winding monologue about Islam, immigration and halal certification.

Hanson was a legend among the Reclaim Australia crowd; her very presence was a sign that theirs was a legitimate, righteous cause, and her persistent effort to return to politics gave credibility to the idea that their gatherings might just translate into something real.

It was right place, right time for Hanson, who supported the movement all the way up to 22 November 2015 – around the time she was gearing up for her latest run at federal politics. Reclaim Australia was attracting larger crowds than ever and the Canberra leg of the national protests marched to the steps of federal parliament chanting, 'Aussie, Aussie, Aussie!' There the marchers were called on to vote for Pauline Hanson at the next election, a show of loyalty the senator from Queensland would repay after settling into her Canberra office by inviting the organisers, failed ACT independent candidate Daniel Evans and Tina Mason to private One Nation functions.

Even among anti-politicians, some habits are worth hanging on to. It's just good politics.

* * *

By the time the Perth rally kicked off, the counter-protesters were nowhere to be seen. They had moved from down the hill to a small courtyard around the corner to be closer to the Reclaim Australia rally, and the police had cornered them in a bottleneck where they couldn't be seen by the television cameras. From then on they were invisible.

As the speakers took their turns, I moved through the crowd to get better photos. Twice, volunteer security grabbed me aggressively by the arm or shoulder to ask who I was and whether I had been 'cleared'. The third time it happened, we exchanged words.

They were two speakers in when I noticed something strange happening at the back where the UPF were hanging out. A young Muslim woman wearing a hijab was talking to the United Patriots Front; members of the group had seen her moving through the crowd and pulled her aside so Chris Shortis, one of Blair Cottrell's lieutenants, could lecture her on the superiority of Christianity to Islam and why her prophet was evil.

It was a surreal scene, as the speeches raged in the background and a Muslim woman listened patiently to the hulking figure of Chris Shortis. By then, my friend with the camera from the independent media had circled back around and was trying to strike up a conversation.

'This is the free exchange of ideas, man,' he said.

Only, from where I stood, it looked more like Shortis was doing all the talking. I shrugged off the photographer and moved in closer to listen, but the wind had started to pick up as the sun beat down. All I could get was snippets, stuff about 'deviant multiculturals' and 'the UN' and 'we will not bow to supremacy'. Another guy filmed the whole thing and when it was all over, the UPF asked for a photo with the woman. She was too polite to say no.

So, the core leadership of the UPF gathered around the Muslim woman in their midst and smiled for the camera. One man gave her bunny ears. Later, they would post the image to their Facebook page, saying they had 'educated her'.

As she went to leave, I asked for an interview and we went down the hill to find somewhere quiet to talk. Her name was Rahila Haidary, she said. She was a twenty-year-old university student, and if anyone out of all the people here really knew anything about terrorism, it was her.

After all, she had been just six years old when the Taliban wanted her dead.

* * *

Rahila Haidary started life as a headstrong little girl in a rural village in Uruzgan, Afghanistan. They were happy years, for the most part, until 2001 rolled around and the Taliban took over.

Rahila was too young to understand what was going on then. Her family were Hazara, an ethnic group considered outsiders by other Afghans, distant relations of the people left behind by the Mongols and those who passed through on the Silk Road. To top it off, they were Shia in a Sunni land, and for that the Taliban considered them heretics.

A six-year-old girl couldn't possibly understand all this, couldn't possibly know that people just like her had been butchered and persecuted by the Pashtun majority, or how the most extreme among them belonged to the Taliban.

All she knew was that it was unfair for the Taliban to ban all girls from attending school. She had been going to class before the Taliban, so why couldn't she go now? It didn't seem right.

Without telling her parents, she dressed as a boy and went to class anyway, but as soon as she walked in the door, every boy in the place knew what was going on and started to whisper. It didn't take long before their teacher caught on and threw her out. That same afternoon, the local Taliban leader met with her father to deliver the message that the choice for his daughter was exile or death, and he had to decide.

Rahila's father sent her away to Quetta, Pakistan, a way station for ethnic Hazaras on the run from the Taliban. It would be five years before the rest of her family would follow. As the American presence in the country eased, the Taliban turned their attention from hunting American troop carriers back to hunting the Hazara, and people were ending up dead.

Her father relocated the whole family to Quetta, and not long after, he disappeared one night. Everyone thought he was dead.

No one knew what happened to him, until the day he called. He had escaped into the mountains and made it to Australia by boat. He had been there, in a detention centre, for some time. Now he was calling to say he was safe, he was alive.

It was Rahila who answered the phone, and when the voice of his little girl reached him, her father had no words.

All he could say was that the family was safe now. He had done it for them. He had done it all for her.

In 2011, Rahila came to Australia and made a life. She enrolled at university and volunteered with Unicef.

I asked her what she thought of the group up the hill.

'They go straight on the Koran,' she said. 'If the terrorists read the Koran and interpret it in the wrong way, they become terrorists. That's also what these people are doing.

'I can't actually differentiate between them.'

After that I asked for a photo, but as I started to shoot I didn't notice that the rally had ended. The crowd was streaming down the hill and a large, bloated man in a blue Australia cap approached us from behind.

He had seen Rahila, a real flesh-and-bone Muslim wearing a genuine, bona fide headscarf, and me taking photos of her. The first time he spoke, it was an incomprehensible grumble of words. Then he repeated it so we could hear.

'Fucking Muslims,' he said to Rahila. 'Think you can just go anywhere you like. Fucking terrorists.'

He said something else I didn't register, but by then I didn't need to. It was hot. My temper was short. I had spent the day being carded by volunteer jackboots in a public space and told to put away my camera. All day, I had been hearing how 'everyone was welcome' and Reclaim Australia was all about the 'free exchange of ideas'. Rahila's face was steely, but betrayed a look of worry bordering on fear. As a rule, I don't take well to having my subjects bullied by outsiders.

'Mate, what's your problem?' I asked, stepping in to redirect his attention away from Rahila.

'You,' he said. 'What are you doing here?'

'I've been at the rally,' I said.

'Bullshit.'

He swore at me after that, told me I wasn't welcome and said all 'you Muslims' were the same.

That's how it was. Rahila's headscarf made her an enemy, and I was a Muslim by association.

I told him to piss off, and he pissed off, mumbling insults under his breath. Then I offered to walk Rahila to her car, which was parked two blocks away. She accepted. Things were getting ugly, and they would turn uglier on the way, when another woman who had been at the rally caught sight of Rahila's headscarf and started yelling as she made her way on the other side of the street, asking Rahila not to cut off her head.

At her car, Rahila said: 'Thank you.'

All I could say was: 'I'm sorry.'

Chapter 19

COLD TURKEY

INDIE ROSE NORRIS DOESN'T QUITE KNOW WHY SHE GOT involved with the United Patriots Front (UPF).

It happened around the time the father of her two children left, taking many of their friends with him. She remembers feeling isolated and alone in those days, and that's when she started to nurse a white-hot anger.

Then there were her parents. When the split happened, they weren't as supportive as Indie would have liked, so she had grown distant from them. Often her closest connection to her parents was their social media accounts and the constant stream of political propaganda they posted. It was weird, she used to think, for people who once were hippies, back when they lived in New Zealand. Her family's closest friends in those days before they migrated to New South Wales were a Muslim family. Maybe it was the culture, maybe it was social media, but with time they had grown political. Pauline Hanson was their woman, and somehow every conversation seemed to find its way back to politics.

Like her parents, Indie had seen what was happening in other parts of the world. She had been seventeen when the Twin Towers burned on September 11 and the image played across every TV channel. Ever since, there had been non-stop stories about war and beheadings in the Middle East, terrorist attacks and suicide bombings and other atrocities far away. As prime minister, Tony Abbott had stood in front of the Australian flag and spoken about ISIS as a death cult. It made her afraid, and the last thing she wanted was for what was happening out there to happen here.

Her fears seemed to have been realised with the Lindt Café siege in 2014, and it was around that time that Indie stumbled onto a video made by a man calling himself 'The Great Aussie Patriot'. His name was Shermon Burgess, the then future founder of the United Patriots Front. He spoke with confidence and seemed to know a truth about Sharia law and terrorism and Islamic migration. He didn't talk about these things like an activist or an academic; he spoke plainly, in ways ordinary people could understand, and as Indie Rose Norris peered into his world through her computer screen, she believed him. The idea that he might be wrong or dishonest did not occur to her. His passion and his certainty were enough, and the community of people he was building around him through social media gave her somewhere to channel her anger into outrage and made her feel like she was doing something right.

Before long, it wasn't enough to just watch videos. She wanted to do more. She wanted to get involved, and her chance came when Burgess put up a post saying he was looking for a designer to help out with his logo. She sent him a message and, with that, she found herself in daily contact with him. That's how she made the transition from rank-and-file to insider.

This kind of access afforded a certain level of respect. People started to know her name and she became an administrator of the United Patriots Front Facebook page. They invited her to secret Facebook groups, while other women took note of her status and suddenly made contact. Some wanted to be friends, some just looked at her with envy and wanted to replace her.

In gaining recognition and respect, she also attracted the attention of the other side. As her name was thrown around the UPF page, the left side of politics started to learn about who she was, and in turn Indie Rose Norris learned that there was a whole group of people out there who despised everything the United Patriots Front were doing and, by extension, despised her.

It was something she couldn't understand. From where she sat, the men of the UPF were just the 'typical guy next door'. They were ordinary guys who said they wanted to serve and protect, men who would step up and defend you when you needed defending. When the left said she was a racist and a bigot too, just like the rest of her new friends, it drove her further into the hands of the UPF.

'You don't see it in yourself,' she says. 'The only people you surround yourself with are telling you it's okay, telling you you're doing a good job. There's a constant stream of ridicule from Facebook, so you cut yourself off from anyone who is critical. You surround yourself with people giving you a pat on the back for that attitude.

'And when you're on the right, anyone who disagrees with you is a straight-up "leftist" or a "leftard". You're not even able to open up your mind to the idea that they may be a person who just doesn't want hate in the world.'

A change started to take place within her, one she barely registered. Before the UPF, she would walk past a Muslim in the street and not think twice. With the UPF, she became hyper-aware of their presence and began to think of them as a threat. She became openly hateful, she says, and without meaning to, her kids began to learn from her. On one occasion, her son watched a Muslim woman get out of a car in Bundaberg and said something about shooting her. It was a moment that sickened Indie. She was in pretty deep, but she wasn't so far gone to know that was wrong and from then on she took steps to isolate her kids from everything she was doing.

Her involvement with the UPF would last under a year, from the moment it was founded until Australia Day 2016.

'All I had to do for it to end was disagree,' she remembers.

During that period, she had been put in charge of the group's finances and given the job of organising their logistics. If the men were out fighting in the streets, the few women in their ranks were kept behind the scenes, booking their flights and running the crowd-funding campaigns that funded their travel.

The end began when she met in person a man she had recruited into the UPF and with whom she had started a social-media romance. Online he had been a warrior, but in the flesh he was a worn-out old man who had no shame in telling her about his criminal history and the allegations of sexual assault other women had made against him.

When she took that information to the rest of the UPF, asking whether they were okay with someone like that coming into the group, they said they were fine with it. That wasn't good enough, she thought, but when she pushed the matter, they told her to shut up.

'Get back to what you do best,' Blair Cottrell told her over the phone. Later, he warned that if she went to the media, he wouldn't be able to control what would happen next.

It was a moment of truth. These were men Indie had passionately defended against stray accusations of criminal activity. People had accused Cottrell of having a Hitler fascination, and individual members of the group had histories of rape and sexual assault. Until that moment, she had thought that people were just throwing mud, hoping it would stick, and she never believed a word. Only now did she start to question what she was doing.

'These guys who were supposed to be some kind of perfect Australian men to protect us all from raping Muslims, some of these guys had actually done that,' she remembers. 'Some of those guys had done these things, so how could they stand up and question all these people? All these other human beings?'

* * *

Christmas 2015, when Indie Rose Norris moved house, she lost a big box of items, including some of her children's artwork. They weren't worth anything, but it was a sentimental loss and she put up a post on Facebook asking if people had seen it. Some of those on the left who monitored right-wing activity online made fun of her, but one activist, a feminist, contacted her to ask, 'all bullshit aside', was she okay? Did she need money?

Indie didn't need money, but this was the first time she had spoken to a person from the other side, and they were actually showing an interest in her wellbeing. As they talked, the part of her mind that had been conditioned to dehumanise her critics slowly started to wake to the idea that the left were people too, with their own thoughts and feelings. With time, the conversation continued until that person invited Indie to a group chat that included a Muslim woman, and there a dialogue began. It was something special, Indie thought, and she decided to do the same thing with her side of the divide.

It was a mistake. One of the women added to the group chat scrolled back through the conversation and realised what was going on; she took a screenshot and passed the image to Blair Cottrell to show the traitor in their midst.

Indie became a non-person. By that time, Blair Cottrell had taken over the UPF and created a strict code of conduct. Any contact with the left side of politics was the mark of a traitor, and the strategy for dealing with traitors was to undermine their credibility. They were to be made an example of to stop any information contradicting the UPF worldview from breaching the echo chamber and reaching other followers.

'Blair [Cottrell] had a set of rules where he said, if you're caught talking to the left, you'll be punished in the biggest way possible,' Indie says. 'And I went holy shit, is this what I'm a part of? I've lost all of my freedom. I can't even talk to my family or I will be shamed. I remember reading that and freaking out, going holy shit this guy is crazy.'

After the UPF decided she was a traitor, they sprang into action. For them, it was damage control. As the person who ran their website and handled their finances, she had access to information that could be damaging to them, so they needed to act fast. A digital lynch mob mustered and videos started to appear online claiming she had been a 'leftie infiltrator' from the start; her personal details were posted online and the whole world was invited 'to skin her alive'.

A torrent of threats flooded her phone and social media. There was no escaping it. Every time she logged on, or checked the screen, there was another message from someone hoping she would die or promising to make it happen. Sometimes they threatened her with rape. Sometimes people sent her photos of her children along with their names and promises to hurt them. Naked photos of her were published online, along with threats to send them to her family and any remaining friends she had. Every day there was another Facebook page telling the world that she was a 'lying whore', or worse. Every time Facebook would zap one, three more would appear. The phone calls, the texts, the messages – it went on every hour, of every day, for months, like a screeching wall of white noise and hatred.

At the time, she was living in a small town in New South Wales and her first instinct was to turn to the police for help, but the country cops were out of their depth. They had no idea who Blair Cottrell was and had never heard of the UPF. They just thought she was nuts.

With no one else to turn to, she contacted the activists she had met online. They helped put her in touch with someone who could provide emergency housing. Indie took her kids and went to ground on the outskirts of Melbourne while she worked out what she was going to do next. Again with the activists' help, she contacted the Victoria Police and worked with officers who had been face-to-face with the UPF at political rallies. In the courts, she took out restraining orders to get her images taken down from social media and force the loudest voices calling for her to be punished to back off.

It took disappearing completely for the UPF to let her go. She moved back to Queensland, changed her number frequently and pulled away from Facebook entirely, for a time. The threats only really stopped coming in February 2017, but every now and then someone from the UPF goes out of their way to remind their followers what happens to traitors. There are even fewer now that the UPF has had its Facebook page taken down entirely.

In a lot of ways, the UPF and the people who follow them are the very things they hate, Indie says. Now she's out of it, when she looks back she thinks of them as no different from the terrorist groups they claim to oppose.

'They don't have access to tanks,' she says. 'If they had access to those things and it wasn't policed so well, they'd become a terrorist organisation.'

And if she has nothing nice to say about her ex-comrades, she doesn't have kind words for the other side, either. Some of those who run websites that track extreme-right figures refused to take down her profile, but they at least let her tell her side of the story. Others were just plain unforgiving. Just because she quit the UPF didn't mean she was welcome on their side of the fence, they told her. As long as she lived, they would remember.

If they will never forget, neither will Indie. She will always remember the attacks, the venom. Hatred and bullying, she says, transcend political boundaries. It's something she's seeing everywhere lately. Every time she turns on the television, she sees another story about how divided the world has become. With Donald Trump in the White House and Pauline Hanson in the Senate, the feeling seems to be that everyone picks a side and those who refuse get blown away in the crossfire.

There was even a story a while back about some kids in Geelong who stole a phone from a young Muslim girl and bullied her, she remembers. When Indie read it, she thought to herself that if her kids ended up like that, she would never look at them the same, knowing they were capable of that kind of hate. It's why she sat them down and told them what she had done, and what she had gone through. She explained how she was lost and is now finding her way back. Most of all, she taught them the importance of thinking for themselves.

That's the moral of her story, she reckons, and maybe by telling it, other women can learn something from her. Or perhaps there's some kind of wisdom there for whole communities who find themselves pushed to extremes and standing on the edge. Radicalisation is a form of bankruptcy: it happens gradually, and then suddenly. Waking up to the realisation you're involved in something ugly is never easy. Not everyone has the strength to walk it back.

Indie Rose Norris did, and now all she wants is the cliché: the little house with the white picket fence and happy kids. But the legacy of her time with the UPF still haunts her. Her personal finances are shot, and because she used her personal account to manage the UPF's money, the department of PayPal that deals with money laundering started to ask about the sums moving in and out of her account.

Then there's the security issue. Life may be getting better for Indie Rose Norris, but the savage burn the UPF ran on her still has her afraid to go outside. She still has trouble sleeping. She still lives in fear that someone might hurt her children.

'I really want to be normal, boring little me,' she says. 'I want to be a mum, I want to be happy – I still haven't got my happiness back.'

It's why a lot of members won't leave the UPF, she says. During her time with the group she met a lot of lonely, angry people who don't truly believe all that the UPF say or do. There's just something about feeling correct, despite all opposition, that soothes personal misery and loneliness. Social media seems like a cure at first, but only ends up feeding the isolation. The other voices from the void tell you to keep going, to hit harder, and eventually they are all you have left. Getting out means giving up everything, so sometimes it's safer to just stay in.

Not Indie, though. She was stronger than the UPF, strong enough to defy them and then strong enough to get out. Life after the UPF means she finally has a shot at something better. She has always been bright, but in Year 8, her high-school bullies drove her out of an education and straight into a job in hospitality. If that hadn't happened, she thinks she might have liked to have been a vet and worked with animals.

Now she's correcting that mistake. She's thirty-three and has just enrolled in university to study nursing. It's her chance to help people, she says, and maybe it's a chance to start something new.

Maybe, on this path, she might even find her white picket fence.

Chapter 20

EAST OF EDEN

NO BABIES ARE BORN IN GATTON, PASTOR JAMES HAAK SAYS, and the place is changing fast. Of the thirty-five years he has been a preacher, the last ten have been spent in Gatton in the Lockyer Valley, a little over an hour out from Brisbane.

Even he admits it's a long time in one place for a Lutheran. The pastors of his denomination tend to be itinerant by profession and work on a call system. Somewhere, out there, a congregation finds itself in need of a shepherd and puts the word out, then a pastor somewhere else who has been feeling the need for a change hears the call and hits the road.

Pastor James hasn't been feeling the need to move on for a while now. He's happy right where he is. The last time he did, he was leading a congregation in rural South Australia, out north near Eudunda, when he got word that the congregation in Gatton needed someone to take over.

He was born out that way, in Toowoomba, a little further west of Gatton, to a farming family who put the church and sport at the centre of their lives. He had come of age in the region and when he was old enough, he left as the early eighties came around, heading almost as far south as a person could go and ending up in Adelaide, where he joined the church and studied scripture at the seminary on Jeffcott Street.

Moving to Gatton meant coming home. Out here work is hard to come by, especially in the surrounding townships, he says when I ask what life is like here. People generally work the farm, or work a checkout at the grocery story, get into the public sector or find a job at the aged-care facility. Not everyone's doing it tough, and there is a real sense of community here, but that's about it for stable employment, and the best shot anyone caught in the middle has of making a better life for themselves is to move away.

Pastor James's son is one of them. He's a software engineer, and he moved away to Brisbane, where he's living with his long-term girlfriend, a Vietnamese woman the pastor describes as a 'lovely girl'. His daughter is still at home for the time being. She just got back from working on an avocado farm in Western Australia with a couple of French and Taiwanese girls in the country on working-holiday visas. She's not one to settle down, he says, and chances are she'll move away too, eventually. There's nothing really here for young people, he says.

That's just how it goes, though. That's change. As for the pastor and his wife, for now they are staying put. She's a teacher in the school and he's got the congregation, though even that too is changing. Once it was 'massive', the buckle on Queensland's Bible Belt, a legacy of the German missionaries and colonists who came to this region a long time ago to make a new life and spread the faith.

'The church was built in 1978,' Pastor James says. 'And they'd fill it. Every Sunday.'

These days, though, the same trend that's winding its way through all religious denominations is eating away at Gatton's Lutherans. Like the other churches, Pastor James's flock are greying and thinning. They've still got 400 people on the books, he says, and about 135 who worship regularly. On some days they can still fill the hall, but the decline here is the same as it is everywhere.

It's not just religion, either. The same thing is happening to all aspects of community life in a place where life on the land was everything, and that goes part way to explaining why the Lockyer Valley is deep Hanson country. Here, one in five people voted One Nation in the Lower House at the last election, and one in three of those voting in Gatton cast their lot with Hanson. This makes the place a lynchpin at the next state election according to Griffith University's Dr Paul Williams, who says that were One Nation's warriors to wrest the valley back from the Liberal National Party (LNP), they will have what it takes to move on the rest of Queensland.

Whether that happens depends on where the LNP decides to preference One Nation. They're getting desperate these days and the two men who will be making the decisions for the upcoming state election, LNP President Gary Spence and state party leader Tim Nicholls, still remember how Labor put them last in preferences at the previous election. Neither have they forgiven them. If they end up placing One Nation higher on the ticket, the minor party could go on to take half a dozen seats across the state and become powerbrokers in the new parliament, with all the media attention that would bring. That would give them a foothold, Dr Williams says. Anything else would just be a bonus.

* * *

One Nation has a lot riding on Gatton. Traditionally, the party has always ruled from the town at the west edge of the Valley. One Nation's former party leader Bill Flynn held the seat until 2004, when Ian Rickuss (LNP) took it from him. Rickuss spoke the language of One Nation and the old National Party, and his muscular approach to politics made One Nation redundant.

His rule went unchallenged until the moment he announced his retirement and One Nation sensed opportunity in the vacuum. That's why there's a billboard facing incoming traffic back out on the highway with Pauline Hanson's face plastered two metres high, next to the image of Jim Savage, One Nation's former Queensland President and a man they parachuted in from the Sunshine Coast to run for them.

In a lot of ways, Savage was a good choice of candidate. Once the fix was in, the local LNP branch had sensed opportunity and, somewhat predictably, moved to paint him as an outsider. Savage wasn't from Gatton, they said, and didn't have roots in the local farming community. When a reporter from the *Queensland Times* asked Savage about it, he coolly spoke about his two decades spent as a farmer in Beaudesert, Queensland. It also helped that he had experience in the oil and gas sector, working between Australia and Papua New Guinea, making it hard to attack him on industry issues. His Filipina wife, meanwhile, offered a crude but effective defence against any possible charges of racism. Where necessary, he could talk about cracking down on boat people for as long as he needed, and should any further charge of racism crop up, he could then talk about his long-running battle to adopt his nieces who had been abandoned by their parents back in the Philippines.

Savage's only real opponent was Jim McDonald, the successor candidate to Ian Rickuss. If Savage was a good choice for One Nation, McDonald was the best possible candidate for the LNP. He was a local councillor with years of experience and a cop who had grown up in Toowoomba, joined the force when he was seventeen and spent fifteen years in Gatton as an officer before taking charge of the Laidley Police for the past decade. He was clean-cut, with strong local connections and a long history of public service.

With four new seats being created and the switch to full preferential voting, there was no way of knowing how things might play out, which was pretty much the story for the rest of the Queensland state election. Odds were the Labor government would be returned, but it was impossible to know what kind of position they would be in given that the polls were showing support for One Nation holding firm, or even growing, particularly in the far north.

It's even harder to get an early sense of which way people are leaning. Mention the word 'reporter' to some locals and they want nothing to do with you. The reputation of the fourth estate is so low in these parts, it's hard to get a One Nation supporter to speak on record even when the pastor makes the introduction. The only thing worse to be than a reporter in Gatton, it seems, is a Labor politician.

Instead, it's left to the pastor to do the talking, and judging by what he says, it seems to me there are two things you need to know about Gatton and the surrounding area: everything it has, and everything it has lost.

There's a new cultural centre in town, and an aquatics centre, and a new airport has opened up. The University of Queensland runs an agricultural campus down the way, but it's mostly self-contained and the students keep to themselves. The soil all around these parts is rich, black and alluvial, making it one of the most fertile regions in the country and among the top ten most fertile in the world. It's why they call Gatton 'Australia's salad bowl' and every harvest the caravan park swells with the backpackers who come over on working-holiday visas. By a quick count, there are at least seven separate churches in Gatton for a variety of denominations in a community of over 7500 people, and there's talk of adding a mosque to replace the Islamic community centre behind the grocery store that services about seventy people regularly. At least three of the doctors at the town's hospital are Muslim.

Then there's everything they have lost.

It used to be that each family got by on about 30 to 40 acres each. They worked the black soil and fed the country. In the lean times, between harvests, they made a little extra money working as tradesmen and labourers around the place, and for the most part it was a good, humble life. Then the fertile soil of the 'salad bowl' became a valuable commodity and the farms went corporate. The parcels of land were sold off one by one and aggregated into bigger entities, while the families who used to work them pulled up roots and left. Mechanisation took away much of the regular farm work, and those who couldn't find anything left the area, or fell idle.

Some found work in food processing, but the butter and cheese factories that used to dot the landscape closed or were amalgamated. They used to can beetroots out this way too, but the last cannery closed down a few years back and while there has been a plan in the works to start up a locally owned facility, it hasn't happened yet. It's a similar story for the local hardware store, a Mitre 10, which closed down in 2016 and hasn't been replaced, despite an ongoing plan to set up a Bunnings. The latest cause of worry is the local dairy industry, or what's left of it. It has been under siege from the supermarket duopolies, which have been squeezing producers for all they're worth. It didn't help either that in 2014, 75 per cent of the state was hit by drought, including Gatton. While the drought classification was lifted for Lockyer in 2015, around the time One Nation was once again becoming active, the thirst had spread to 80 per cent of Queensland.

That's Gatton, but the further out you go, the more the struggle deepens. Leave the highway behind, drive away from those places where the irrigators operate and you'll find it. These are the smaller satellite communities and homesteads. Inside these towns there are the offices dedicated to a rural plan to bring start-up culture to the regions, and the magnificent Eagle Rock Café in Laidley, a '50s-style American diner. Life for them has never been easy, though it's never been bad.

It's the same story all over Australia, the pastor says. Gatton's story is no different and those who have been around long enough remember how it was. Some have genuine reason to be angry, some are just nostalgic for a past that isn't coming back and was never that good anyway. Not everyone feels that way, but there are enough people feeling like they've been neglected, no matter who's in power, that it's starting to show. If those people weren't voting for One

Nation, they would be parking their vote with the LNP, but when that happens the Coalition tends to get comfortable with the idea that they've got Gatton sewn up, and they stop delivering.

Rightly or wrongly, what it all comes down to is a sense of control and the quality of outcomes. That's what's got some people feeling like they're at the end of the line.

'It's about who makes the decisions and where those decisions are made,' Pastor James says. 'When your decisions are not made by you, they're not made in your town, you can't get angry at the boss. So, who do you take it out on?

'When you don't appear to be listened to by politicians and businessmen and someone comes along and says let's have a go at changing something, that's powerful.'

* * *

The pastor prefers not to have much to do with politics. The closest he has come is getting to know Ian Rickuss, a member of the congregation. It's not the Lutheran way to preach in the pulpit. Sure, Joh Bjelke-Petersen made a public display of his faith when he was around, but in matters of men, Pastor James subscribes to the notion that God works through the law of the land.

For the most part, though, the pastor is optimistic about the future and his faith is clearly fixed to the inevitable triumph of hard work and endurance. The government has just signed free-trade deals with places like China, he says, which should give the local dairy farmers a way out, somewhere else to sell their milk. The backpackers and itinerant labourers who move through Gatton with the seasons bring their money with them and make the whole place feel more diverse and alive. There's both a settled refugee community in town and a Muslim community, but despite the racist stereotypes and what some media commentators insist, crime is virtually nonexistent.

That said, in May 2017 there was a shooting. A loner with a criminal record and a violent history turned his machine gun on a police officer manning a roadblock just outside town.

The shooter was a white man.

'You know, we don't have riots on the street on Saturday evening between the Africans and the rednecks hiding down the back somewhere,' Pastor James says.

None of this means the pastor doesn't have his own complaints. There might be plans underway to build big box businesses, and new facilities like the aquatics centre are 'wonderful', but for now Gatton is still a town where no babies are born and you can't buy a hammer. Every expectant mother has to make the thirty-five-minute drive west to Toowoomba, or an hour back down the highway towards Ipswich, to give birth because the Gatton hospital doesn't have specialised paediatric services. Anyone who runs into trouble is pretty much on their own. Any woman looking to leave a violent husband has nowhere to go, nor do those who fall into homelessness. Sometimes the police call to say they've got someone who needs somewhere to stay on short notice and could the pastor help. When it happens, he does his best. Sometimes he puts them up in the hall for a few days or finds them a temporarily unoccupied unit, but it's only a short-term fix.

Life in the country might have always been like this to some degree, but as time goes on the big cities feel further and further away.

It's this that is at the heart of One Nation's revival, he says, at least in these parts. Even if he doesn't necessarily agree with it, Pastor James can certainly understand it. It's why the young ones leave and the old ones stew in the memories of what they've lost. What city people write off as a poisonous nostalgia is more a deeper fear of isolation and vanishing. It's an outrage at watching everything you've known be erased. Every crop sown and every harvest wrought. Every storm weathered. Every drought endured.

'You know,' Pastor James says on the way out, 'there's a saying around here. It's quicker to drive to Brisbane than it is to make the trip back to Gatton.'

Chapter 21

FOOTNOTES

MITCH FOLBIGG DOESN'T REMEMBER HIS FIRST BRUSH WITH history. He was eighteen and drunk on the streets of Newcastle the night he staggered up to *Sydney Morning Herald* reporter Margo Kingston and straight into her book about Pauline Hanson's failed 1998 campaign.

It was Hanson's second visit to Newcastle that night, and she was giving a speech at the Entertainment Centre. The police had thrown up a barricade to keep her supporters and counter-protesters from fighting in the street. Kingston had retreated outside to chain-smoke cigarettes and wait out the storm, while Mitch had withdrawn from the barricades, thinking it wasn't worth it because of the good-behaviour bond he was on. He ended up buying her a beer and together they talked. In two pages she summed up his life at that point in time, painting a picture of an angry young man grappling with a world in which the old certainties of his father's generation were gone, or going.

Mitch was a footnote in Australian history, an extra in the background of an unfolding drama that wouldn't even merit a mention in the credits at the end of the film. Almost two decades on, Mitch lives in Woodridge, Queensland.

'What do you want with me?' he asks when I find him online. No hello, no small talk.

I state my business, telling him I've been trying to track him down and I want to write about him. He was mentioned in a book, I say, but he has no idea about that, so I send him an extract.

'I have to warn you,' I tell him. 'I'm not sure you're going to like what was written in that book.'

* * *

Mitch doesn't hesitate to say he was a thug. It's one of the first things he tells me over a beer at Hotel HQ in Underwood. These days he tries to stay out of fights and away from the law, but back then it was a different story.

Growing up, his family was blue collar. His father worked on the railway and the family moved around a lot. They would never really settle down until just after Mitch started high school, when they moved into Warners Bay, New South Wales, and put down roots.

Even then, they were rough days. His father was an inspector for the state rail company and a good part of his job was cleaning up the bodies when someone stepped in front of a train, or an accident happened. Back then no one really understood post-traumatic stress, and Mitch watched his father turn to the bottle to cope.

It was around this time he watched his best friend die. He doesn't want to talk about the details, other than to say it was bad. Really bad. He says it matter-of-factly, like that's just the way it was, like there's nothing really to it. It's the same way he talks about a lot of his life, such as how he never made it through school. The teachers said he had a 'bad attitude' and a problem with authority. He'd get bored and frustrated, and then he'd lash out, try to hurt someone. He was defiant to a fault, maybe because he had to be, so he only made it halfway through Year 9 before the school administrators sat him down and gave him a choice: leave or be expelled.

So, Mitch left. He was working then, flipping burgers at McDonald's for the minimum award rate, about $15 an hour, he remembers, though he thinks he could be wrong on that one. Newcastle's economy was starting to slide around that time. The rust had set into the steel industry and the old myth of a job-for-life was a legend of the past. That's when he started to turn into his father.

Mitch was hanging out with older kids then. They all drank, just like his dad, so Mitch drank too. When they went looking for trouble, so did Mitch. If there was a fight to be had, he would be the first to throw a punch. He loved the violence and didn't care about the consequences. Today, he's not exactly sure why.

All Mitch's friends smoked weed, so he smoked weed too. He was thirteen and a half when he tried his first joint, and he coughed his lungs up and fell asleep. After a while, he used it to self-medicate. Whenever he got worked up or angry, he'd light up and calm down. That's how the addiction started.

And when his friends started to smoke 'harder stuff', he started to smoke harder stuff too. He says from the age of fifteen it started to get really bad.

'Back then, you got paid and you spent it on drugs,' he says.

He's not sure where the racism came from. It didn't come from his family; for all their problems, they were fairly accepting of other cultures, he says. He just had this idea of the way the world was, the way it worked and how it didn't need to change for anybody. He hated Aboriginal people for the handouts they got. He hated immigrants for the competition they brought to the job market.

He was around eighteen when he decided he wanted to learn about politics. His father voted Labor, his mother voted Liberal, but Mitch wanted to make up his own mind. He started to learn about the different political parties to see what they were about, and then one day he saw an advert on the television for One Nation. He decided he'd go down and hear what they had to say. That was the first time Pauline Hanson went to Newcastle.

She spoke to something in Mitch that day. She said a lot of things he agreed with, a lot of things he thought other people were too afraid to say. Pauline had no fear, though. He respected that, and the more she talked, the more she made the world make sense.

'Pauline was a lovely person,' he remembers. 'Had a lot of time to talk and discuss what she was trying to say. If you had questions, she was more than willing to answer them. David [Oldfield] on the other hand was just a complete dropkick. He was short, straight to the punch. Didn't really want to hang around too much.'

Still, Mitch got both of them to sign a T-shirt, and he joined up to the youth wing of the party. From then on, he followed her with interest. He loved that she was so in-your-face and made people mad. He hated the smarm of the major parties, their stale rhetoric and their blanket opposition to something he thought was obvious.

The second time Pauline went to Newcastle was different. Mitch had moved up to Queensland to live with his grandparents and get away from his 'bad habits'. He got a job, and didn't have time to get in trouble, but he didn't know anyone there, so he went back to Newcastle and fell straight back into his bad habits. He was working on a construction site with a friend's dad then, and the day Pauline was due to speak they started drinking early, around 3.30pm.

Mitch had got into a fight with counter-protesters earlier that day, at a shopping centre where Pauline was supposed to appear but didn't. He turned up to the venue where she was supposed to speak that night. There were counter-protesters there too and the police had set up a barricade to try to separate the different groups, but one of the One Nation people had walked through the middle of the counter-protest chanting 'Pauline for PM', starting another fight. Mitch joined in.

He was pretty drunk by then, but he wasn't so far gone that he forgot he was on a good-behaviour bond. It wasn't worth it, he thought, so he left and walked into Kingston's book.

Not long after that visit by Pauline, Mitch marked adulthood with an overdose. When he opened his eyes, he saw his mother watching him, and then he caught the gaze of his father.

'He said to me, "Don't you ever do that to me again,"' Mitch remembers. And from that moment on, he never touched the 'harder stuff'.

* * *

Around the time One Nation fell apart, Mitch married. He was twenty-four and married the mother of his first child when they had a second kid on the way.

Mitch didn't do it out of love, he says. He did it because he wanted the child to take his name so the family line could continue. It was important to him then, but it was dumb and as 'nasty' as it sounds, he says, though he's not trying to hide it. He was not a good man, not a good husband, and not a good father.

'Looking back on it now, it was a mistake,' he says. 'But I got two beautiful children out of that, two step-children and a step-grandchild.'

No home life built on those motives could last. Mitch might have got married and he might have had kids, but he didn't really have a family and eventually he and his first wife separated on what Mitch says were amicable terms. The two children, however, were removed and now live with Mitch's parents in Newcastle.

What you might call the turnaround began almost three years ago, when Mitch Folbigg learned he had a black history.

It started when he wanted to find out about his roots. He had been learning about his family history, and when he dug a little deeper he discovered that his mother's great-great-grandmother was Aboriginal and belonged to the Darkinjung people. There was a similar story on his father's side too, but there were no clear details about the connection. These family secrets had been kept for at least two generations.

'The first thing I thought to myself was, I'm a fucking hypocrite,' he says.

It was a discovery that forced Mitch to re-evaluate a lot of things he thought about the world. He wanted to learn more, so a friend of his, an Aboriginal man, took Mitch to the bush, where he met an elder who offered to educate him about his heritage.

'He stripped me back to nothing and rebuilt it all,' Mitch says. 'Growing up, I always thought the Aboriginals got everything they wanted and got the long end of the stick, but when I stopped and looked for it, it was the other way around. There was so much they do not get that they deserve. Education for the Aboriginal community, especially out in the middle of nowhere, is very poor. The government doesn't want a lot to do with them, leaves them to their own devices and then decides to raid them when they're drunk.

'Everything I had known up until then was wrong.'

Mitch, though, won't go so far as to say it changed him. He prefers to say he's grown.

'I'm very proud to say I am a black man,' he says. Mitch even has an upside-down Aboriginal flag tattooed over his heart.

'The way people are hiding their Aboriginal heritage, it's almost like they're in distress and when you're in distress you put the flag upside down,' he explains. 'A lot of people are hiding their Aboriginal heritage as if there's still something wrong with it.'

As much as things have changed, they've also stayed the same. Mitch still supports Pauline Hanson, he's still anti-immigration, and these days he doesn't trust Muslims. He still drinks, and he still smokes, but he doesn't touch drugs anymore. He doesn't share his politics with his kids, either.

A little while ago, he went back to Newcastle to apologise to some of the people he went to school with for the way he treated them. They were a little stand-offish at first, he says, but when he explained himself, they listened and now they're close.

In a couple of weeks he will marry his fiancée, Nickie. Nickie is no fan of politics, and doesn't pay attention to it unless it's got something to do with her kids, one of whom is on the autism spectrum, just like one of Mitch's kids. Mostly, she keeps Mitch in line, they both agree. He has become less rude and less arrogant in their time together, and her friends aren't surprised. Their nickname for Nickie is 'The Pitbull'.

'Because they know that if I'm pushed, I go for the throat and won't let go,' Nickie says.

The pair met online and started to talk when Mitch accidentally video called her one night and she accidentally picked up. Once she said hello, there was nowhere to hide, and the pair got to talking. Soon it became a nightly thing. One day, her nine-year-old appeared on camera and introduced himself. He loved *Star Wars*, and so did Mitch. The two became fast friends.

That's how Mitch got himself a family.

* * *

The way Mitch sees it, politics is a lot like high school. There are the bullies, like Donald Trump, a guy who runs his mouth on Twitter, and everyone else is too afraid to stand up to him. Call them wimps, call them suckers, call them whatever you want, that's the rest of the world right now. The kind of politicians Mitch respects are those who can call out the bully, take a punch, and throw one back. They're people like Pauline Hanson, or Derryn Hinch.

'They're not afraid to say you're a scumbag and you shouldn't be sitting there and doing this,' Mitch says.

If they fail – well, then they're just like every other politician who has come before them.

That said, Mitch hasn't had much time for politics lately. Ever since he met his fiancée, he has been getting his life together, and that has meant his only priority has been family. It doesn't leave much time for anything else. The only time he tunes back in is when they're talking about something that may affect the kids.

He's quick to say he hates the major parties, though. One year they'll promise one thing, then the next they'll do the opposite. When Tony Abbott was prime minister he was talking about how we need to lower taxes. Now the government is talking about how they have to raise them.

Mitch doesn't pay tax, so it doesn't bother him. What bothers him is the inconsistency. It's always one thing, then it's another. Which is it?

Who knows?

In fact, the last time politics did anything for him, personally, was the bonus Kevin Rudd gave people as a way to keep the economy going in the middle of the Global Financial Crisis. On the issues, ask Mitch what he cares about and the first thing he names is immigration. His feeling is that immigrant labour is undercutting Australian jobs, a sense that hasn't changed since he was a kid, and he likes that the federal government has been cracking down on the flow of refugees. He would like to see them crack down further.

Then he moves away from Nickie to go smoke a cigarette and I join him. As he talks, I think about how at this point, politics and pollsters have usually made up their minds. The pollsters decide they have what they need and move on to the next question, or the next caller. The left side of politics decides Mitch is a racist, while the right thinks all it has to do to win Mitch's vote is crack down hard on refugees, then sit tight.

Listen for a little longer and Mitch will tell you he's thirty-seven now and in the past five years has had both a heart attack and a stroke. He'll tell you he doesn't like what he's been hearing lately about how the federal government wants to change the education system in ways that are going to make life harder for his kids in the long run, and he certainly doesn't like how they're dragging their feet on reforms to the National Disability Insurance Scheme. Mitch survives on a Disability Support Payment while his kid, his fiancée's kid and his fiancée's best friend's kid are all on the autism spectrum.

What it comes down to for Mitch is accessibility of jobs. He is too physically and mentally broken to work, but he wants his kids to do better. These days, he's more positive than he's ever been, he says, but even he is finding it hard to see how that's possible when every entry-level job seems to require some level of qualification. It's why he has no faith in politics, or politicians, and about the only thing that's going to change his mind on that account are serious results.

'Words are one thing, actions are another. As I tell my kids, the one thing I did learn off my dad as we were growing up, is that I can say sorry a million times but whether or not I'm actually sorry, and whether my actions say I'm sorry, is a completely different story altogether. The Liberals and Labor and even the independents can sit there and say, "We're going to do this, we're going to do that." But put it into action. Show me you are doing that. Then I might be swayed.'

Until that time, he's going to keep voting for Pauline Hanson, he says. It's why he's glad she's back. At her best, she gets right up in their face and she gives them hell.

'She'd have to pass away,' Mitch says when asked what it would take for him to stop voting for her. 'Or something major would have to happen, like she'd have to kill a puppy or something.'

* * *

Two weeks later, in June 2017, something big happened. In an address to the Senate, Hanson was giving a rambling speech on matters of education when she took a detour to talk about disabled kids in the classroom.

> I hear so many times from parents and teachers whose time is taken up with children – whether they have a disability or whether they are autistic – who are taking up the teacher's time in the classroom. These kids have a right to an education, by all means, but, if there are a number of them, these children should go into a special classroom and be looked after and given that special attention. Because most of the time the teacher spends so much time on them they forget about the child who is straining at the bit and wants to go ahead in leaps and bounds in their education. That child is held back by those others, because the teachers spend time with them. I am not denying them. If it were one of my children I would love all the time given to them to give them those opportunities. But it is about the loss for our other kids. I think that we have more autistic children, yet we are not providing the special classrooms or the schools for these autistic children. When they are available, they are at a huge expense to parents. I think we need to take that into consideration. We need to look at this. It is no

good saying that we have to allow these kids to feel good about themselves and that we do not want to upset them and make them feel hurt. I understand that, but we have to be realistic at times and consider the impact this is having on other children in the classroom.

We cannot afford to hold our kids back. We have the rest of the world and other kids in other countries who are going leaps and bounds ahead of us. Unless we keep up a decent educational standard in this country we will keep going further backwards and backwards, and our kids will not be the ones who are getting the good jobs in this country. They will be bringing in people from overseas and filling positions in this country that belong to our children. Our education is very important, and I feel that it needs to be handled correctly and we need to get rid of these people who want everyone to feel good about themselves. Let us get some common sense back into our classrooms and into what we do. Like I said, One Nation has spoken to many areas. Have we got it right? I hope we have got it right, because it is very important.

Hanson provided no facts, nor any numbers on the average number of disabled children in classes. She cited no research on best practices when it came to education and disability. Reporters heard a call to segregate disabled, and particularly autistic, children into special classrooms because they take up too much of the teacher's time, 'hold our kids back' and threaten to pull down education standards.

To Mitch, it sounded a lot like a doomed puppy, at least at first. It was reported as if Pauline Hanson wanted to segregate his kids into separate classrooms, which was 'bullshit', he said. If true, he had just found the limit of his support for One Nation.

'I have kids with Autism Spectrum Disorder, and being in mainstream schooling is the best thing for them,' he said.

As we were talking, the story was going viral, with Labor and the Greens sensing a wedge issue and joining forces to attack Hanson. Across social media, the outrage grew. People pointed to the cruelty of directing 'tough talk' at kids who already struggled. I agreed with them. I knew this was not the first time Hanson had pushed for an exclusionary policy for the disabled. In 1998, the party had released a policy on disability going into the election that was largely a footnote among everything else that was going on. When Crikey dug out the document, it called for a reassessment of 'community-based care' for people living with mental and physical disabilities, suggesting instead they be placed in 'centre-based care'. While it stressed that people with disabilities should be 'respected for their individual worth and dignity', it justified its policy by saying: 'Much of the community concern at present stems from fear that residential areas will suffer from inappropriate placement of intellectually disabled people with anti-social behaviour.'

The outrage to her 2017 speech was bigger than Hanson expected, and the night the story broke she posted a video to her Facebook page, claiming she had been taken 'out of context' by a journalist with the *Courier-Mail* who had run a headline that read: 'Pauline's plan to get rid of autistic kids'. Hanson encouraged her followers on social media to lodge a complaint with the paper.

I wanted to know what Mitch thought as a parent with autistic children, so I sent him Hanson's video, which included her speech.

'Okay, yeah,' he said. 'What she said is all about having a huge group of children with Autism Spectrum Disorder in one class. I get what she is saying now.'

This was the IKEA-model of political speech: Hanson gave her listener the pieces and left it to them to self-assemble. To Mitch, the critical information was the phrase 'if there are a number of them'. This contextualised her comments, he thought. It was a similar response he would have in mid-August when Hanson pulled a stunt by wearing a full burkha on the floor of the Senate. As the newspapers and political personalities denounced her for the stunt, Mitch applauded Hanson for her audacity in challenging the country's political leadership in one simple move.

Everything else, as far as Mitch was concerned, was media spin. As far as Hanson's autism speech went, those among her critics who thought they had scored a king-hit were overestimating their reach. The attack on Hanson might have done something to bloody Malcolm Turnbull by association, but did little to peel away Hanson's supporters.

They were still preaching to the converted.

Chapter 22

THE TROUBLE WITH WESTERN AUSTRALIA

THERE WAS A SORT OF GLEE WHEN THE FIRST OF THE VOTES started to come in on 11 March 2017. Colin Barnett had survived eight and a half years as a Liberal Party strongman in the west, a beacon of stability and certainty even as five prime ministers were put to the sword in the halls of Parliament House.

But when the polls closed and the count was broadcast to the nation that Saturday, Barnett's enemies knew he was done.

It was the final act in an election drama most people had paid no attention to. For the entirety of the campaign, there had been only one real issue: the $40 billion in red ink the state government of Western Australia had racked up post mining boom.

The man behind it all was Colin Barnett. He was the guy who sold the country on the idea of a never-ending mining boom. He had run a 'business-friendly' state government and handed out permits to anyone who had come back from the desert thinking they had struck gold. Anyone could make a fortune out of the boom, it was said, and if you weren't involved, you had to be crazy or stupid, and if that was true, you didn't deserve one anyway.

No conversation held in Western Australia could escape that $40 billion question. Every time a politician spoke about funding for health care or education, it was connected to the boom. The Roe 8 protests that dominated the south of Perth were connected to Barnett's drive to sink every dollar made out of the boom into infrastructure.

Even the return of One Nation was set against this backdrop. The election had been called at a time when Trump was president, Brexit was happening and One Nation had risen from the ashes at the federal election to take four Senate seats in parliament. It was thought the resentment that breeds when an economy begins to slide would feed the rise of the far right, and everyone wanted to know whether Pauline Hanson was about to echo, note for note, her big brother Donald Trump and his rise to power within the US Republican Party.

But when the initial tallies showed that One Nation had only managed to pull 4.93 per cent of the vote in the Legislative Assembly – instead of the 13 per cent that had been expected – journalists, commentators and political heavies immediately seized on the result as proof, in their thinking, that Australian pragmatism and reasonableness had won out.

Somehow, Australia had managed to buck a global trend. The whole thing was a colossal 'flop' and everyone from

Federal Cabinet down breathed a collective sigh of relief. One Nation had been crushed, and nobody had to seriously grapple with the notion that they were a credible threat.

Western Australia was One Nation's first big election since the 2016 federal election when they surprised everyone by running and winning seats. It was a state far from home where they were building campaign machinery from scratch. Pauline Hanson throwing Rodney Culleton under a bus had raised some eyebrows, and the sacking of the craziest candidates from their ranks was alienating some of its most fanatical supporters. James Ashby might have grown frustrated at having to deal with people who weren't always reliable, but they were the raw material that kept One Nation moving, and it was his job to work with what he had.

And then there were the gaffes. In Kalgoorlie, the local candidate had spelled the town's name wrong on the campaign posters that bore his mugshot. In her interview with Barrie Cassidy, Pauline herself had praised Vladimir Putin as a strong leader and role model for Australian leadership, she had said vaccinating your children was a matter of personal choice, and she told Western Australia she would fight to give the state a better share of GST revenue, even at the expense of her home state of Queensland.

Talkback radio tore her to shreds.

Most of all, there was the preference deal with the Liberal Party. For short-term political gain One Nation had formed a temporary alliance with the embodiment of the establishment and in doing so had compromised their narrative of representing an alternative to the major parties. Hanson was being wined and dined by Michaelia Cash in what came to be seen as a sweet embrace of the Liberal

Party, and anyone who cared to check the numbers would notice One Nation tended to vote with the government.

And yet, despite everything, despite all the gaffes and the screw-ups and the incompetence, One Nation still managed to secure 4.93 per cent of the vote, an improvement on the 3.99 per cent support they received in the Western Australian Senate vote at the 2016 election. More than that, the party had only contested 35 of 59 seats in the Legislative Assembly but had still landed 7.5 per cent of the vote in the Lower House, averaging 8 per cent in the seats it targeted and 10 per cent in country areas. By the time 72.3 per cent of the vote was counted, One Nation was still on track to land two seats in the Legislative Council, and by the time it was all said and done, it would end up with three. While that wouldn't give them the balance of power, it would give those candidates four years to learn the rituals of holding office in the west.

In conventional terms, the whole thing was a write-off, but then, to One Nation, convention didn't apply. In the political battle being waged on the national stage, everyone had been reading their actions as if they were a conventional fighting force, when they were more like a guerrilla group operating out in the mountains.

Seen in this light, One Nation starts to make a whole lot more sense. Historically speaking, every time a smaller, unconventional force with more heart than brain first squares up to an organised, professional unit, they do so by the traditional rule book and it gets them slaughtered. Afterwards, the survivors fall back, regroup and carefully rethink their approach. This is the first lesson of guerrilla warfare: the victors decide when they've won, but it's the losers who decide when the fight is over.

The second lesson is that the only goal is to stay alive.

Seen this way, the only surprise to anyone who was paying attention to the result of the 2017 Western Australian state election was that One Nation didn't do worse. With no campaign machinery, no idea and on the verge of civil war, the group managed to double the result they saw at the 2016 federal election, and wound up with three MLCs.

Among the early pundits, the only one to take a measured approach was Junkee's political editor Osman Faruqi, who pointed out that the party had actually built on the share of the vote it received at the 2016 federal election, a better measure for their success than the last time they had run candidates out west two decades ago. Everyone else declared One Nation dead for failing to deliver the clean sweep they expected. Like George W. Bush standing on that deck of an aircraft carrier in front of a banner that read 'Mission Accomplished', the news went that One Nation was a 'flop'. The Huffington Post went so far as to run a screaming headline calling it a 'monumental fail'.

At its core, this reflected a certain kind of Australian exceptionalism, the idea that somehow, some way, the people of this country are immune to the global forces realigning political systems everywhere from the Philippines to the United States. To justify this, some pointed a righteous finger at compulsory voting as a moderating force in Australian politics; others pointed to the nature of our parliamentary system itself, which tends to dilute political movements rather than concentrate them at the centre of power.

Taken together, it's a way of thinking that is, first, arrogant and, second, blind. It allows us to think ourselves immune to a global phenomenon and in doing so makes us less vigilant, letting us ignore what is already going on. It speaks to a narrow worldview that assumes Trump is the only possible result, while forgetting that these same forces also produced Brexit.

All it took in that case was a figure like Nigel Farage to survive long enough for Conservative prime minister David Cameron to give him an opening. That story began with a conversation over pizza in an airport lounge and a months-long political campaign that has been described by Professor Michael Dougan as one of 'the most dishonest' in the country's history. It ended with a political crisis and a rewriting of the international order.

Australia too, it should not be forgotten, has been talking in recent years about holding national votes on becoming a republic, Indigenous recognition and same-sex marriage. At the same time, One Nation and some members of the Coalition want Australia to walk away from the Paris agreement on climate change, or pull out of the UN Refugee Convention. Each presents a distinct opening for a vicious kind of politics to grab the mic and run its mouth on the national stage. In some ways, it already has.

The preference in Australia has so far been to treat the whole problem as if it is temporary, a 'populist moment' that will pass, or has already passed. This lets us pretend nothing is happening and act as if suppressing a peasant revolt through the technical machinery of our electoral system is enough. The implication of this is that it also lets our political leadership off the hook.

If, however, the problem is structural, if wealth inequality deepens, or rises, and alienation from the political process has something to do with it, the problem won't go away, but will continue as someone learns to exploit that resentment in a more disciplined way.

And there is good evidence that Australians are no more immune to populists than anyone else. Our political system seems to be manufacturing populists right now, and they are currently sitting in federal and state parliaments where no amount of technical manoeuvring has so far been able to dislodge them. It's how Tony Abbott became prime minister and why we have seen every effort we made on climate change scuttled. It's why we have watched the rise of the Greens on the left, One Nation on the right and Nick Xenophon in the middle. Hanson is just the latest. If it weren't her, it would be someone else promoting a similar brand of ethno-nationalism.

That's why it's wrong to count One Nation out just yet. Western Australia *should* have sunk them. Their result *should* have been zero. Instead they survived what should have been a crushing defeat to find themselves represented in the new Western Australian Parliament.

Like any good insurgency, Pauline Hanson's One Nation won't stay dead.

Chapter 23

BLACK SWANS AND WHITE QUEENS

THE MAN BEHIND THE COUNTER DOESN'T SPEAK MUCH English.

'Yeah?' he says, with that kind of universal, no-nonsense look that says, *What d'ya want?*

There's a flat-screen television up on the wall and it's broadcasting the state funeral for the cop who was murdered out near Gatton a few days back by a creep waving a machine gun. I stop and watch for a minute, thinking about how his death was used by Pauline Hanson to deflect uncomfortable questions from some SBS reporters about the alleged misuse of party funds.

The guy behind the counter looks at me, waiting for an answer. I get the cod and chips with chicken salt and think about starting up a conversation.

Then I don't. When the Vietnamese family who bought this place moved in, they didn't know who Pauline Hanson was, just that she was famous. That's how they became famous by proximity. Soon after, reporters started to turn up looking for soundbites, artists appeared to give them political artworks and the curious swung by once in a while to dine on fish and potato scallops in the birthplace of Australian fascism.

So I left the guy alone and took my bottled water to a seat on the footpath out front. Most people, I figure, come here to look inward, to stare in at the warm yellow walls and the soft-drink cans on the shelves, and soak in the glorious irony of a Vietnamese refugee family taking over a chip shop once owned by the woman who raised her voice over fears about 'being swamped by Asians' and hordes of boat people.

I came here, instead, to look outward. To see what Hanson saw every day when she came to work here on the outskirts of Ipswich, when she cast her gaze out from over her shop counter and onto the world.

Turns out, it ain't much. Just a thoroughfare for cars and a house with a weathered red roof set against an infinite blue sky.

Moving further out completes the picture. This is a neighbourhood that has known struggle. All around here is the familiar feel of the weathered white picket fence and the little signs of the Australian wealth divide that exists but is never obvious. There are the houses where the lawns are mowed regularly and those with the car bodies rusting in the driveway. There are the angry young men walking around feeling like life is rigged against them but not knowing why or how to express it. About half of all people living around here never finished high school, according to the Census data available at the time of writing. Unemployment, the numbers say, is hovering at about one in ten. That was roughly the same number of people who voted for One Nation in this part of town.

As it goes with most outer-city proto-ghettos, it's the people who make a place worth living in. Sitting at another table right here is an old man nursing a bottle of Coke. He's thin, a pile of wrinkles and white hair peering through glasses at what looks like a technical document in front of him. A young woman, blonde hair, blue eyed and tough as nails, keeps coming in and out of the hairdressers next door to take care of one chore or another. Then there are the two tradies who turn up on their lunch break, one old, one young. The old guy goes to move the car, leaving the young guy in hi-vis to wait for the order. There is the hiss of a Coke bottle opening for the first time.

That's it. For all the years Hanson worked this joint, hers was an ant's-eye view of the world, with all the limits and constraints and distortions that entails. Everything seems bigger with that kind of perspective. Everything makes you afraid. The newspaper headlines seem louder, so too does the television. And when everything seems so big, and it feels like there's so little to go around, losing some is always going to feel like losing a lot.

It's not hard to see how Hanson got traction here. If the political process is a matter of deciding who gets what, when and in what amount, this part of the world isn't exactly top priority, though these days Ipswich central is getting a little more attention and there are certainly worse places to be. The First Nations people of this country live in levels of poverty the rest of the country likes to pretend don't exist in a developed nation. It's something Aboriginal peoples have been saying for a long time now, but Australia only really pays attention to it when someone like photojournalist Ingetje Tadros, a Swede, turns up and embarrasses us internationally by taking her camera to Kennedy Hill.

That is a different conversation, though, and a whole other history. Besides, none of this is a contest about who has it worse with a winner-take-all outcome. That's Hanson's shtick. The world is far more complex than that, and sometimes these different stories interlock in unexpected ways.

It's why the curiosity with the 'white working class' doesn't help. The reality for the United States is that the white working class didn't elect Trump: a few white working people in key districts swung the vote in his direction. The same term does not translate well to Australia, either. We can try importing the idea of the 'white working class' and applying it here to make a prediction and we would inevitably end up wrong. This applies to the impulse to reduce the whole phenomenon to 'economic anxiety' or put it all down to racism. People don't lose their job and vote for One Nation, and racism alone only makes sense if Hanson were the only populist in parliament.

Economic problems, after all, are felt as cultural problems. Class may frame an issue, but race contours or deepens it. Social media then transmits the result. People navigate the rich interplay of these social drivers as best they can and sometimes they are crushed by them. Whatever happens to them in the end, they can always still vote and at the ballot box, people look for someone to vote for, not something to vote against.

While it's fashionable to wave it away, the role class plays in this cannot be ignored. Class, to be clear, is about power. You're working class if you have no control over when you work, how much you work or how fast you work, and you know that you'll be the first to go if the company decides to trim the fat tomorrow, making your future insecure. On this spectrum, the more freedom you have moves you further up the social hierarchy. If you can take holidays, buy the latest iPhone and have some notion that tomorrow is always going to be better than today, you fall into the middle and upper classes. A truck driver who works for a company is middle class by this definition, but a self-employed truck driver who's still paying off the loan he needed to buy his rig, even as it depreciates in value, is someone the company kept on contract because it didn't want to deal with superannuation and regular wage rises and holiday pay. That driver is working class and, depending on the details, even working poor.

It can be a hard life at the bottom, but so long as everyone is able to get by, that's not a problem. It's why Australia built the social safety net just after World War II at a time when public debt was 120 per cent of GDP and later converged on a system in which the Australian government took care of the big stuff like health care and education. As we poke holes in our safety net, the wealth divide widens and people find themselves priced out, banished to the edges of major cities where they are stigmatised, or working on contract in a poor region as they grow to feel increasingly isolated.

That's when their personal misery and bitterness grows, and the facts don't matter anymore. All they see is another group somewhere who have it better off; all they hear are sneering putdowns – and when someone promises to hit them back, they listen.

To lift a line from political economist Mark Blyth of Brown University, democracy functions when the losing side of an election continues to see their quality of life get better, despite the result. When this social pact breaks down, so do the old certainties. In that way, the growing US wealth divide sowed the seeds of Trump's electoral success; dog-whistle politics, misogyny, social media and lies fertilised it; and a common touch brought in the harvest.

That's the United States in a nutshell, but Australia has its own version of this global trend that is slowly taking apart established political parties across the industrialised world, pretty much anywhere there is a stagnant working class and a slipping middle. Whether it is Millennials versus Boomers, the propertied versus the renters, city versus country, east coast versus everyone else, or poor versus rich, the gap between those with and those without is growing. This is what World Bank economist Branko Milanovic was driving at when he published his now famous 'Elephant Chart', which plotted the change in real income for every person in the world and visualised a situation in which the biggest losers were the middle-income earners among industrialised economies. In this kind of environment, populist alternatives on both the left and the right start to look attractive.

Australia does not exist in isolation, and Hanson is very much a product of this trend. Halfway through writing this book I read David Marr's Quarterly Essay *The White Queen*, which mapped out the structural changes in Australian politics around the issue of race and retold Hanson's history. Marr painted in numbers the poisonous nostalgia that has helped Hanson rise again, like some fumbling Darth Vader staggering from the depths of the Australian subconscious. Using numbers from the 2016 Australian Election Study, Marr showed that Hanson drew her support from women, the elderly, those without university qualifications and those in trades – who were all angry at the government.

These people, those without education, who have savings and mortgages, are people with something to lose and are exactly the people you would expect to be swinging right at this moment in history. Australian household debt is the highest it has ever been at 189 per cent of income and more than 123 per cent of GDP. Meanwhile, wage rises are no longer keeping pace with the cost of living, and the amount of spare money Australians have to throw around fell between December 2011 and December 2015, and has yet to fully recover. The country might have had a record period of growth, but there is more to the story than just the headline.

These dynamics are at play behind the growing preference for independents and minor parties across the country. Lower quality of life, higher levels of debt and a discredited political establishment are what push people on both sides of politics to the margins because there is a sense that something isn't fair. In between, all the traditional antagonisms deepen. Those on the right feel like it's got something to do with race and immigration, so they vote for Pauline Hanson over the LNP. The other half of the story, those on the left side of politics, think it's got something to do with rich people, and they vote Greens over Labor.

Among them are the populists, Hanson included, that bogeyman of careerist bureaucrats and the professional political class who more often than not throw the word as a stinging insult. Populism, however, is radical democracy and a by-product of neglect or indifference by the status quo. It works by taking different interests and binding them together against a common enemy, a coalition of the underdogs united, despite the traditional antagonisms or apparent contradictions between them, along a clear overarching theme. It is possible to trace how this played out in the United States where Trump promised voters a radical vision for a better America, and then positioned Hillary Clinton as the one stopping them from having it.

Populism in itself isn't a bad thing, but it's what you combine it with that makes it potent. Mixed with the left, it focuses on those with money and power. Blended with the right, it takes aim at immigrants, refugees and enemies of the nation. Keep it in the centre and everyone ends up unsatisfied. Put it in a coalition and its worst impulses are tempered, allowing it to do some good by pushing for reform in those areas that sorely need it. Give it majority rule, things can turn ugly.

And just like elsewhere, it is happening to Australia. Aside from Senator David Leyonhjelm, a standout in origins and outlook, and the Christian right representatives of Lucy Gichuhi and Cory Bernardi, the loose alliance of Senate crossbenchers and Lower House independents have been putting the hurt on the major parties for the better part of a decade and, in some cases, have even dictated the agendas of governments. These people may not embrace the label 'populist' for its stigma, but it accurately describes their politics. Among them, there are enough populist independents sitting in federal parliament that, taken together, they form the fourth-largest voting bloc after the Greens, who are themselves dealing with an internal challenge mounted by Senator Lee Rhiannon, another populist who responds directly to the will of her base.

These people may not be able to form government, and Hanson especially will never become prime minister, but with the trend towards government by coalition and a persistently fractured Senate, populists are powerful. Each represents a regional blend on the same general theme, operates on the same basic principles, and will often work with each other at the expense of the major parties. They are, in a manner of speaking, a decentralised, emergent political party.

The story of Hanson, then, is the story of the breakdown of political parties, even as the trend at the moment is to put the root causes all down to a momentary lapse in common sense. A changing culture does have something to do with it, but so does class, wealth inequality and a growing underclass. Holding one up to the exclusion of others allows all perspectives to converge on one safe interpretation of the facts, one convenient narrative that enables us to keep believing that Australia is special.

If it is true that somehow Australia is immune to global populism, Tony Abbott, himself a populist, would never have been prime minister. If true, Malcolm Turnbull's promise, made with much confidence during the 2016 federal election, to clean out the Senate and restore 'responsible government' to the nation, would have been kept. As the record now shows, it didn't happen and the lower threshold made his problem worse. At the last election Labor found itself with fifteen Lower House candidates winning from second place off preferences, the largest number in its history, while the Liberal Party failed to win the majority it desperately sought. Meanwhile, over 1.4 million Australians, or more than 9 per cent of 15.7 million eligible voters, did not cast a vote in the Lower House at the last federal election, and 8.1 per cent of people did not vote in the Senate.

Now the independents and minor parties have a deeper beachhead into parliament, with the potential to build on their position. At the time of writing, projections by the

Australia Institute suggest One Nation has the potential to expand to eight federal seats, eclipsing the centrist NXT and rivalling the Greens.

What this speaks to is the deeper sickness within the major parties, one that extends to both players. Each side views the other, and their supporters, as a hopeless lost cause, or some hostile enemy, and this division is amplified with every attack meme and partisan news column. As the battle rages, the winner-takes-all approach to politics unfolds, and everyone loses. Instead of working on the kind of quality-of-life issues that win support and have the potential to unite people with different interests or antagonisms, major party political figures grow increasingly discredited with every helicopter flight to a golf course and every interview with Leigh Sales that is nothing but filler.

Some of the results have been a 34 per cent swing against the Nationals in favour of the Shooters and Fishers in the Orange by-election and five prime ministers in ten years. It's how the whole of Melbourne has fallen to the Greens with Brisbane slowly following suit, while flyover country South Australia is being consolidated by Nick Xenophon and Pauline Hanson's rebellion moves from the countryside towards the centres.

It is possible to discount this, to say that voting for a minor party or independent candidate is a lottery, as there's no way of knowing where your vote will end up. This may be true, but then politics itself has never been a perfectly rational process. If it were, there would be no way one in three voters in the Lockyer Valley would have grown angry enough to cast a vote for One Nation and against the wellbeing of the Muslim doctors who serve their community. Nor is it totally mad. Just before One Nation grew active, drought spread across Queensland and a debt crisis was pushing farming communities, in some cases, to open revolt against their creditors, which goes some way to explaining one plank in One Nation's populist coalition.

Hanson herself is something else entirely, a product of random chance that has rewritten the rule book.

Acknowledging the role of random chance in any event is not something that sits well within the Australian psyche. As a people, we respect mastery and skill because we like the illusion of certainty or repeatability. Putting something down to chance is to make it less threatening, or less significant. It's why we rely on numbers to soothe our angst in the face of the unknowable.

Problem is, politics itself is a deeply human activity and cannot be forecast in numbers. No matter how big the sample size, some outcomes are impossible to predict, especially in something as complex as the Australian political system. These are 'Black Swan events', things so statistically improbable they could not have been predicted in advance because there was no real historical precedent, but end up having an extreme impact that people try to rationalise in the aftermath.

It is a mistake to pretend like they don't happen, just as it would be a mistake to underestimate their seriousness. To paraphrase Nassim Nicholas Taleb and Mark Blyth: when the barn door swings open to reveal a farmer holding an axe, no one is more surprised and confused than the turkey that has lived its life in perfect happiness and knows, for sure, tomorrow will bring more of the same.

No amount of data, for instance, could have predicted that one racist letter to a Brisbane newspaper would have triggered a series of events that saw Pauline Hanson pushed onto the national stage, leading to a fundamental restructuring of the right in Australian politics with long-term consequences for issues as diverse as Aboriginal land rights, refugee policy and even climate change.

Nor did Hanson go away. The natural response of both major parties at the time, to use the political system to suppress the event, did not stop it from playing out. All it did was make things worse in the long run. Two decades on, Hanson now holds four seats in federal parliament and has the ear of the Prime Minister, with the Queensland election yet to play out at the time of writing. Political wisdom said she was finished as of 1998.

What's new is that this time around Hanson has been joined by other populists, though it would also be a mistake to make a straight comparison between them. Each may be a little rough around the edges, but most have largely taken their job and their responsibilities seriously, kept their eyes on the long game and mostly played by the rules.

As much as Hanson is a veteran, she is also new in that ecosystem. She is a woman of broad strokes, with an aggressive, short-term, transactional approach to politics and an intuitive feel for exploiting people's arrogance, anger and hurt, all in the right place, at the right time. Her game relies on everyone else thinking they're too smart to be had: her supporters think they're too smart to be made suckers by powerful people, while her opponents think they're so clever she doesn't have a chance, and as proof they always point to the numbers. Where they overlap, Hanson thrives. It's what got her elected in 1996, and why one in three people in the seat of Blair voted for her in 1998, despite her ultimate defeat on preferences.

And anyone who thinks it's crazy that she's back, that there's no way the same hustle could work twice, would be wrong. In the world of confidence tricksters, the term is called 'reloading', a type of scam run on a person who has already been ripped off, which makes them more vulnerable the second time. One victim who gets had in an email scam is contacted by another victim who suggests chipping in for a private investigator. A man who misses a shot on a carnival game is told he shoots like a girl, so buys in for another round. An investor is burned on a sure thing but, as their stockbroker explains, there is inherent risk in any deal and, to make up for it, they'll give them a tip normally kept for VIP clients.

This is not to say that Hanson is grifting or that she is illegitimate. I have no doubt that Hanson believes in the message she brings, whatever it may be. These are just the mechanics of why she is back and why no one should expect scandal to sink her. It didn't in Western Australia, despite the headlines announcing she had bombed. Nor will the contradictions in her policies take her down, or the internal civil war that is going on behind the scenes of One Nation. That's not what the people who vote One Nation care about. They may not believe half of what Hanson says, if they're being honest, but that is not the point. All that matters is that she connects, on some level, with their frustration, their resentment, their need to be recognised as clued in to what's 'really going on', and that she seems to scare the living hell out of the bastards. The louder the outrage, the sweeter the sound.

That's what people mean when they say 'she listens' and 'they don't'.

This does not guarantee that Pauline Hanson, herself, will stick it out. Hanson tends to misfire. At heart, she might not really be capable of capitalising on any of it, nor are her party officials or parliamentary staff. It may well be that Australia's independents and minor parties will hold their own, or that One Nation are again pushed out through procedural wizardry. At any time, One Nation could schism after one purge too many, or Hanson might decide she's had enough with the ongoing investigations into her party's finances and conduct, that she's getting too old for the flak she has to deal with every single day and may just want to bow out. Without her name, One Nation is nothing.

Anyone who says they know what is going to happen is wrong. There is a growing body of people who can't see a future for themselves, or their children, in those parts of the country that struggle. These people don't believe a single word that escapes the lips of their political leaders. They are sinking on the rising tide, or have been made to watch from the shore, but they can still vote.

If not for Hanson, then someone else. Anyone else.

It's why I have a problem when people argue that this is all just a 'moment'. In doing so, they usually point to the recent French election which Marine Le Pen lost, signalling to some the high-water mark of this 'populist revolt'. Yet a third of the French public still thought it was okay to vote for fascism rebranded. Those people are going nowhere unless something changes in their lives and their fortunes. Suppressing it won't make those people go away, just as changing voting laws to eliminate the ability of minor parties and independents to find office won't do anything to change the reasons people are voting that way in the first place.

The only way to take the pressure off is to go back to basics and put quality-of-life issues at the heart of public debate. Building stadiums might make for flashy vote winners, but aside from a few temporary construction jobs, it does nothing to build the robust loyalty needed to endure the appeal of populist movements, of which we can expect more. Putting doctors in a community so people don't have to drive forty minutes for medical care is also a vote winner that makes everyone's life better in the process. Taking them away breeds resentment.

The left, arguably, has an easier time of this, as the architects behind institutions such as Medicare, though Labor has largely abandoned the bottom 30 per cent to pursue the aspirational middle ever since 1996, when it let Howard falsely claim that the 'battlers' had switched sides. In doing so, Labor became complicit in poking holes in the social safety net. The right side of politics will fare worse. As long as the mining boom brought in the money, they could ride it to electoral success. As soon as it stopped, the commitment to austerity and free trade at all costs moved the Coalition to take up the scalpel more often than the hammer, while the biggest legislative fights on the Coalition side of the divide have mostly been cultural and ideological struggles *against* issues such as same-sex marriage and unions.

So, what, exactly, are Labor and Coalition supporters voting *for*?

I hope events prove me wrong about all of this, but as far back as the 1960s, Donald Horne was pointing to an Australian political class that was so uninterested in global events, so blinded by ideology and comfort, that when global became local, they were always taken by surprise.

My fear is that nothing has changed.

POSTSCRIPT

As this is being written, the full bench of the High Court is sitting down to hear lawyers argue over what they should do to resolve a minor constitutional crisis involving the citizenship status of several ranking political figures.

It's been months in the making and now that the country waits to find out the fate of a group that includes the Deputy Prime Minister, everyone is wondering what will happen next.

So far the judges have been hinting that those whose citizenship status is in question will stand or fall together, with no regard for their individual circumstances. True or not, the end result of their decision will be the same. Sooner or later, the independents and populists will have another crack at taking some measure of power, either in a by-election, or at a federal election. Some have already been positioning themselves to do just that. Almost from the moment the constitutional and political crisis began, Tony Windsor started calling for Barnaby Joyce's head by joining the High Court case against him and pushing for a by-election in the seat of New England. Nick Xenophon, meanwhile, was caught up in the crisis owing to the former status of Cyprus as a British colonial possession, but ducked the verdict entirely with the announcement that he will quit the Senate to run in the upcoming South Australian state election. In doing so, he upset the carefully laid plans of both the South Australian Labor government and the Liberal opposition, who would now have to pick up an extra seat for every one claimed by Nick Xenophon's newly formed party, SA Best.

In the background to all this, the internal populist frictions within the established parties have continued. Tony Abbott, the political insurgent, has been organising the backbench of the Liberal Party against any effort to support renewable energy while soaking up the media attention offered by the same-sex marriage survey. On the Labor side of politics, the ACTU has found a new voice in the figure of Sally McManus and her denouncements of neoliberalism, which may drag the party further to the left. Nor are the Greens immune, with the emerging Left Renewal faction sniping at 'Tree Tory' party leader Richard Di Natale.

Some figures within these groups are already defaulting to 'talking populist' in order to ward off any potential challenge. The most extreme example of this so far has been the candidacy of Clare 'Burnsy Sanders' Burns for the Victorian state seat of Northcote in a critical upcoming by-election. *The Australian* reported that Labor had sunk $500 000 into her campaign to fend off a challenge by the Greens; in spite of this, Burns still dressed her office front window in the DIY hand-written signs and campaign material of financially precarious grassroots movements the world over.

If true, it's another triumph in style over substance, another exercise in pure smarm. Dropping an F-bomb in conversation or sticky-taping a hand-written sign to your campaign office window is not people power and those jaded enough to want for an alternative see through it at a glance. The only thing these people hate more than a professional politician who says nothing, is a professional politician – or an aspiring one – pretending to be something they're not.

As journalist Gideon Haigh pointed out after reading an early version of this manuscript, if the professionals keep letting technocrats do their thinking for them, the independents will endure: 'The parties have outsourced all ideas other than those involved in winning elections. Ideas are now bought off the rack, as it were, from lobbies or think tanks. The independents, by contrast, *do* transact in ideas – often stupid ideas, but their own, and that commands a certain respect.'

Right now, though, tacticians within the major parties have been running the numbers ahead of the next federal election, which will see half the Senate seats being contested, and are again talking about how the Upper House will be cleared out. Derryn Hinch is likely to go, along with Lucy Gichuhi and David Leyonhjelm.

Maybe they will, maybe they won't. Who will pick up their seats if they do? No one can say for sure, but across the board the established parties are trying to hold their finely balanced coalitions together in an effort to stop their vote share from shrinking, and in their attempts to please everyone, they are pleasing no one.

Whatever happens, if the major parties have any hope of holding off the independents for the long haul, they will need to find something to fight for.

And they *are* capable of doing so. There is no finer example of this than when South Australian state premier Jay Weatherill ambushed federal energy minister Josh Frydenberg during a press conference in March 2017 on renewable energy. In the lead-up to the exchange, Frydenberg had been beating up the state government over its renewable energy policy. The moment the federal minister planted his feet on South Australian soil, it set up the perfect confrontation. Even if Weatherill couldn't shake the robotic tone of politics, his dressing down of Frydenberg under the national spotlight meant that for one refreshing moment, a political figure was confronting a threat like an actual human being, by telling his bully to step off.

It wasn't nice; it wasn't statesmanlike, but that was entirely the point. It's why it worked.

Make no mistake though, the message here is not that switching to a raw communication strategy, or enlisting a charismatic leader as a figurehead, will change the trend. The problem has never been the pitch, or the packaging, but the product. So long as people keep answering the question, 'What has politics done for you, personally?' with a blank stare or a distant, abstract memory, they will keep looking for an alternative.

And that means nobody is safe.

Notes on Sources

THROUGHOUT RESEARCHING THIS BOOK, I HAVE HEARD stories of love in the time of Hanson, stories of personal hardship and stories of middle-class comfort. None of these were written. Many One Nation supporters I approached for this work either refused to speak to me, refused to speak on record, or refused to admit their allegiance. It is to those who spoke to me for this book, inside and outside of the political process, to whom I owe a deep debt of gratitude. These are people named, those who aren't and those who couldn't be.

Listed on the following pages are the primary sources used to help construct the profiles in this book and which shaped my thinking. They include books, news articles, documents, statistics and other materials used for backgrounds, primary materials and those works I extract some definitions from.

It was a deliberate choice to not discuss the Alt-Right in the chapter 'Cold Turkey' but instead to focus on the human consequences of those tactics. The preface owes a literary debt to *US Guys* by Charlie LeDuff.

James Ashby didn't respond to my emails, either.

Sources

NEWS MEDIA, COMMENTARY AND ANALYSIS

Alcorn, G., 'The underdog bites back', *Sydney Morning Herald* (online), 19 April 2014 <http://www.smh.com.au/federal-politics/the-underdog-bites-back-20140413-36m7y.html>.

Alonso, J., Interview with Mark Blyth (Transcript published by E-International Relations, 13 August 2016) <http://www.e-ir.info/2016/08/13/interview-mark-blyth/>.

Armitage, R., Harmsen, N. and Scopelianos, S., 'Bob Day: Hundreds of homes in doubt as senator's building company collapses', *ABC News* (online), 18 October 2016 <http://www.abc.net.au/news/2016-10-17/families-facing-uncertain-future-amid-home-australia-collapse/7939842>.

Aston, H., 'Clashes between Glenn Druery and party founder Keith Littler behind sacking', *Sydney Morning Herald* (online), 2 August 2014 <http://www.smh.com.au/federal-politics/political-news/clashes-between-glenn-druery-and-party-founder-keith-littler-behind-sacking-20140801-3czmu.html>.

Blake, S., 'Tony Windsor's regret: not getting to "wipe the floor" with Barnaby Joyce', NewsCorp (online), 26 June 2013 <http://www.news.com.au/national/tony-windsor8217s-regret-not-getting-to-8220wipe-the-floor8221-with-barnaby-joyce/news-story/e00293e95f48cb0180ff567a15522c7a>.

Blyth, M., 'Global Trumpism: Why Trump's victory was 30 years in the making and why it won't stop here', *Foreign Affairs* (online), 15 November 2016 <https://www.foreignaffairs.com/articles/2016-11-15/global-trumpism>.

Brent, P., 'Perilous Pauline', *Inside Story* (online), 10 March 2017 <http://insidestory.org.au/perilous-pauline>.

Brooks, R., 'Donald Trump is America's experiment in having no government', *Foreign Policy* (online), 28 April 2017 <http://foreignpolicy.com/2017/04/28/donald-trump-is-americas-experiment-in-having-no-government/>.

Butler, J., 'Pauline Hanson and One Nation's monumental fail in the WA election', Huffington Post, 13 March 2017 <http://www.huffingtonpost.com.au/2017/03/12/pauline-hanson-and-one-nations-monumental-fail-in-the-wa-electi_a_21880453/>.

Cameron, D., 'Census figures show financial hardship common in Townsville', *Townsville Bulletin* (online), 5 July 2010 <http://www.townsvillebulletin.com.au/news/census-figures-show-financial-hardship-common-in-townsville/news-story/31a5b05f9eb05a87550d871d28e610ca>.

Campbell, R., 'Fact check: Will Adani's coal mine really boost employment by 10,000 jobs?' *The Australian* (online), 31 August 2015 <http://www.theaustralian.com.au/business/business-spectator/fact-check-will-adanis-coal-mine-really-boost-employment-by-10000-jobs/news-story/903c1932738b1d1a1763c74e45f4d7c7>.

Cassidy, B., 'One Nation: Voting patterns show Pauline Hanson's impact runs deep', *ABC News*, 22 September 2016 <https://medium.com/abc-news-australia/one-nation-voting-patterns-show-pauline-hansons-impact-runs-deep-3de0c282ed15>.

Creighton, A., 'Be honest about unemployment – it's above 15 per cent', *The Australian* (online), 22 May 2017 <http://www.theaustralian.com.au/business/opinion/adam-creighton/be-honest-about-unemployment-its-above-15-per-cent/news-story/633ce52659090ab5ff9e0ee2e036aa52>.

Crowe, D., 'Old hand takes firm grip in Hinch office', *The Australian*, 3 December 2016 <http://www.theaustralian.com.

au/news/nation/old-hand-takes-firm-grip-in-hinch-office/news-story/f64e8cc794b7ec9301bcf84dd3e51bc9?login=1>.

Daley, P., 'Jacqui Lambie on home turf: "I reckon I can do 20 more years"', *The Guardian* (online), 27 June 2016 <https://www.theguardian.com/australia-news/2016/jun/27/jacqui-lambie-on-home-turf-i-reckon-i-can-do-20-more-years>.

Darby, A., 'Senator Jacqui Lambie on her rock star status, life as an underdog and why the PM should take her out for lunch', *Sydney Morning Herald* (online), 17 July 2015 <http://www.smh.com.au/federal-politics/political-news/senator-jacqui-lambie-on-her-rock-star-status-life-as-an-underdog-and-why-the-pm-should-take-her-out-for-lunch-20150711-gi9dk9.html>.

Denniss, R., 'Spreadsheets of Power: How economic modelling is used to circumvent democracy and shut down debate', *The Monthly* (online), April 2015, <https://www.themonthly.com.au/issue/2015/april/1427806800/richard-denniss/spreadsheets-power>.

Denton, A., Transcript of interview with Pauline Hanson (*Enough Rope*, 20 September 2004).

Farr, M., 'Tony Windsor – 22 years of exceeding expectations', *Daily Telegraph* (online), 26 June 2013 <http://www.dailytelegraph.com.au/news/opinion/tony-windsor-8212-22-years-of-exceeding-expectations/news-story/fa11d3fff40d9e263e487ce18974a070>.

Faruqi. O., 'Despite the Setbacks Pauline Hanson's One Nation is still a rapidly growing political force', Junkee, 13 March 2017 <http://junkee.com/despite-setbacks-pauline-hansons-one-nation-still-rapidly-growing-political-force/98219>.

Finlay, L., 'High Court confirms Rod Culleton is not a senator – so what happens next?' The Conversation, 3 February 2017 <https://theconversation.com/high-court-confirms-rod-culleton-is-not-a-senator-so-what-happens-next-72349>.

'Former One Nation senator Rod Culleton declared bankrupt', *The Guardian* and AAP (online), 28 June 2016 <https://www.theguardian.com/australia-news/2016/dec/23/former-one-nation-senator-rodey-culleton-declared-bankrupt>.

Hardy, E., 'In Their Own Image: The rise of the launch-your-own political party', *The Monthly* (online), 14 April 2015 <https://www.themonthly.com.au/blog/elle-hardy/2015/14/2015/1428987541/their-own-image>.

Hutson, M., 'Why Liberals aren't as tolerant as they think', *Politico* (online), 9 May 2017 <http://www.politico.com/magazine/story/2017/05/09/why-liberals-arent-as-tolerant-as-they-think-215114>.

Jericho, G., 'To those who claim Australia's unemployment data is dishonest please stop', *The Guardian* (online), 30 May 2017 <https://www.theguardian.com/business/grogonomics/2017/may/30/to-those-who-claim-australias-unemployment-data-is-dishonest-please-stop>.

Johnston, C., 'Federal election 2016: "He will be eliminated." Is this Ricky Muir's last stand?', *Sydney Morning Herald* (online), 12 June 2016 <http://www.smh.com.au/federal-politics/federal-election-2016/he-will-be-eliminated--is-this-ricky-muirs-last-stand-20160609-gpfiz9.html>.

Judis, J.B., 'Rethinking Populism', *Dissent* (online), Fall 2016 <https://www.dissentmagazine.org/article/rethinking-populism-laclau-mouffe-podemos>.

Knott, M., 'Pauline Hanson's One Nation emerges as government's most reliable Senate voting partner', *Sydney Morning Herald* (online), 4 March 2017 <http://www.smh.com.au/federal-politics/political-news/pauline-hansons-one-nation-emerges-as-governments-most-reliable-senate-voting-partner-20170304-guqo6i.html>.

Koch, T., 'The nickel mine that ensnared two tycoons,' *The Australian* (online), 12 December 2015 <http://www.theaustralian.com.au/news/inquirer/the-nickel-mine-that-ensnared-two-tycoons/news-story/12f46054d9afe808bbfc0702ff831957>.

Latham, M., 'Mark Latham: Rise of the outsiders – Trump-style revolution is coming here', *Daily Telegraph* (online), 30 January 2017 <http://www.dailytelegraph.com.au/news/opinion/mark-latham-rise-of-the-outsiders-trumpstyle-

revolution-is-coming-here/news-story/76b16ef69ccb63a3bcab0
d9ec5b3a2b2>.

Leser, D., 'Pauline Hanson's bitter harvest', first published
30 November 1996 and later in *The Whites of Her Eyes*
(1999, Allen & Unwin), republished in 'Good Weekend' via
Sydney Morning Herald (online), 17 September 2014 <http://
www.smh.com.au/good-weekend/gw-classics/pauline-hansons-
bitter-harvest-20140828-109dbf.html>.

Lind, M., 'Now more than ever, we need a radical center', Salon,
20 April 2010 <http://www.salon.com/2010/04/20/radical_
center_revisited/>.

Maccalum, M., 'A Polite Friction: Malcolm Turnbull's attempt
to ignore Tony Abbott while pinching his policies is not
working,' *The Monthly* (online), 12 September 2016.

Maiden, S., 'Roo poo flies in Senator Ricky Muir's "toxic" office of
hangers on', *Daily Telegraph* (online), 2 August 2017 <http://
www.dailytelegraph.com.au/news/opinion/roo-poo-flies-in-
senator-ricky-muirs-toxic-office-of-hangers-on/news-story/2a9
bb12cdac3ee1306c2dd4554c14af7>.

Manne, A., 'Joker in the Pack: On the road with the irrepressible
Nick Xenophon', *The Monthly* (online), November
2015 <https://www.themonthly.com.au/issue/2015/
november/1446296400/anne-manne/joker-pack>.

Mather, A., 'AMWU boss John Short says Pauline Hanson's non-
halal Easter eggs campaign could threaten Cadbury jobs', *The
Mercury* (online), 12 April 2017 <http://www.themercury.com.
au/news/politics/amwu-boss-john-short-says-pauline-hansons-
nonhalal-easter-eggs-campaign-could-threaten-cadbury-jobs/
news-story/0ee30e5c2ba400b090501b25528fc230>.

McDonald, M., 'Pauline Hanson draws hundreds at rally', *Morning
Bulletin*, 19 July 2015 < https://www.themorningbulletin.
com.au/news/pauline-hanson-draws-hundreds-supporters-at-
rally/2710753/#/0>.

Middleton, K., 'Pauline Hanson's plans to expand One Nation',
Saturday Paper (online), 10 December 2016 <https://www.
thesaturdaypaper.com.au/news/politics/2016/12/10/pauline-
hansons-plans-expand-one-nation/14812884004076>.

Mudd, G. and Jowitt, S., 'Queensland Nickel's demise: Yabulu, a relic refinery', The Conversation, 20 January 2016 <https://theconversation.com/queensland-nickels-demise-yabulu-a-relic-refinery-53368>.

Neales, S., 'Farmers forced off their land fight back in Queensland', *The Australian*, 6 December 2014 <http://www.theaustralian.com.au/news/inquirer/farmers-forced-off-their-land-fight-back-in-queensland/story-e6frg6z6-1227146447933>.

O'Brien, L., 'My journey to the center of the alt-right', Huffington Post, 3 November 2016 <http://highline.huffingtonpost.com/articles/en/alt-right/>.

Petitjean, C., 'Ernesto Laclau, theorist of hegemony', Verso Books, 30 April 2014 <https://www.versobooks.com/blogs/1578-ernesto-laclau-theorist-of-hegemony>.

Ravlic, T., 'Exclusive: One Nation breaks electoral rules', *Saturday Paper*, 29 April 2017.

Remeikis, A., 'The arms race for Queensland: How Sunshine State will decide next government', *Sydney Morning Herald* (online), 2 June 2017 <http://www.smh.com.au/federal-politics/political-news/the-arms-race-for-queensland-how-sunshine-state-will-decide-next-government-20170601-gwi8a3.html>.

Rolfe, M., 'Identity crisis: who does the Australian Labor Party represent?', The Conversation, 17 April 2014 <https://theconversation.com/identity-crisis-who-does-the-australian-labor-party-represent-25374>.

Rundle, G., 'Rundle: "Preference whisperer" alleges backstabbing and dysfunction behind Ricky Muir', Crikey (online), 6 August 2014 <https://www.crikey.com.au/2014/08/06/rundle-preference-whisperer-alleges-backstabbing-and-dysfunction-behind-ricky-muir/>.

Rundle, G., 'Clivosaurus: The politics of Clive Palmer', extract from *Quarterly Essay* published in *The Monthly* (online), 26 November 2014 <https://www.themonthly.com.au/blog/guy-rundle/2014/26/2014/1416964947/clivosaurus>.

Rundle, G., 'Rundle: there's no use screaming, the Australian alt-right is already here', Crikey, 2 December 2016 <https://www.crikey.com.au/2016/12/02/rundle-the-australian-alt-right-is-here/>.

Schipp, D., '"Great for the white race"': KKK rises on Trump's politics of hate', NewsCorp, 30 April 2017 <http://www.news.com.au/entertainment/tv/current-affairs/great-for-the-white-race-kkk-rises-on-trumps-politics-of-hate/news-story/ebabe613fe1945de4eb0fe76824df936>.

Schneiders, B. and Millar, R., 'Melbourne's population boom masks Victoria's economic woes', The Age (online) <http://www.theage.com.au/victoria/melbournes-population-boom-masks-victorias-economic-woes-20170630-gx1ses.html>.

Taibbi, M., 'The end of facts in the Trump era', Rolling Stone (online), 8 February 2017 <http://www.rollingstone.com/politics/features/taibbi-the-end-of-facts-in-the-trump-era-w465615>.

Taibbi, M., 'Trump the Destroyer', Rolling Stone (online), 22 March 2017 <http://www.rollingstone.com/politics/features/taibbi-on-trump-the-destroyer-w473144>.

Turner, R., 'WA election: Flux the System micro-party puts up 26 fake independent candidates', ABC News (online), 3 March 2017 <http://www.abc.net.au/news/2017-03-03/wa-election-flux-microparty-running-fake-independent-candidates/8323342>.

Turner, R., 'WA election: Potential conflict over preference whisperer Glenn Druery's Senate job', ABC News (online), 8 March 2017 <http://www.abc.net.au/news/2017-03-08/wa-election-potential-conflict-over-glenn-druery-senate-job/8336948>.

Uren, D., 'Wages may have stalled, but inequality is not rising in Australia,' The Australian (online), 20 April 2017 <http://www.theaustralian.com.au/business/opinion/david-uren-economics/wages-may-have-stalled-but-inequality-is-not-rising-in-australia/news-story/0152537c892aa67ed0f7e7e3c68b1818>.

Vincent, S., 'Eyes Wide Open: What does One Nation senator Malcolm Roberts really believe?' The Monthly (online), November 2016 <https://www.themonthly.com.au/issue/2016/november/1477918800/sam-vincent/eyes-wide-open>.

Walker, J., 'Wrecking ball or mastermind?', The Australian (online), 4–5 February 2017 <http://www.theaustralian.com.au/life/weekend-australian-magazine/enter-stage-

right-james-ashby-still-ruffles-feathers/news-story/
bd79cb7e9589f1b7f809eade8c2e0057>.

Watson, D., 'In praise of Tony Windsor', *The Monthly* (online),
August 2013 <https://www.themonthly.com.au/issue/2013/
august/1375315200/don-watson/praise-tony-windsor>.

Whiteford, P., 'Election FactCheck: Has the Coalition presided
over the most sustained fall in Australian living standards
since records began?', The Conversation, 8 June 2016 <https://
theconversation.com/election-factcheck-has-the-coalition-
presided-over-the-most-sustained-fall-in-australian-living-
standards-since-records-began-60327>.

Wrigley, B., 'John Madigan returns to the tradesman's life after six
years in the senate', *The Courier* (online), 22 October 2016
<http://www.thecourier.com.au/story/4244426/john-madigan-
on-getting-back-on-the-tools-feature/>.

Zhou, N., 'Rent virtually unaffordable for those on low incomes or
welfare, survey finds', *The Guardian* (online), 27 April 2017
<https://www.theguardian.com/australia-news/2017/apr/27/
rent-virtually-unaffordable-for-those-on-low-incomes-or-
welfare-survey-finds>.

'Adani board pushes ahead with Queensland coal mine, chairman
confirms', *ABC News* (online), 6 June 2017 <http://www.
abc.net.au/news/2017-06-06/adani-board-pushes-ahead-
carmichael-coal-mine-palaszczuk-says/8593042>.

'Let's not talk about the constitution: Culleton self-represents
in High Court appearance', AAP via *SBS News* (online),
21 November 2016 <http://www.sbs.com.au/news/
article/2016/11/21/lets-not-talk-about-constitution-culleton-
self-represents-high-court-appearance>.

'Shooting an elephant: charting globalisation's discontents', *The
Economist* (online), 17 September 2016 <https://www.
economist.com/news/finance-and-economics/21707219-
charting-globalisations-discontents-shooting-elephant>.

BOOKS

Bageant, J., *Deer Hunting with Jesus* (Portobello Books, London,
2008).

Halstead, T. and Lind, M., *The Future of American Politics: The Radical Center* (Anchor Books, 2001).

Hartcher, P., *The Sweet Spot* (Black Inc, Melbourne, 2011).

Jones, R., *Ashbygate: The plot to destroy Australia's speaker* (Independent Australia, Sydney, 2015).

Kingston, M., *The Pauline Hanson Trip* (Allen & Unwin, Sydney, 2001).

Savva, N., *The Road to Ruin* (Scribe, Melbourne, 2017).

Watson, D., *Recollections of a Bleeding Heart: A Portrait of Paul Keating PM* (Random House Australia, Sydney, 2011).

Zachariah, L., *Double Dissolution* (Echo Publishing, Melbourne, 2016).

DATA, POLLING, STATISTICS

Anglicare Australia, 'Rental Affordability Snapshot', Report, April 2017.

Changes to discretionary spending source from Australian Bureau of Statistics, 5206.0 Australian National Accounts: National Income Expenditure and Product: Table 1. Key National Accounts Aggregates: Real net national disposable income per capita: Chain volume measures – Percentage.

Department of Employment, 'Small Area Labour Markets', March Quarter, 2017.

EMRS, 'State Voting Intentions Poll (Tasmania)', poll, 6 March 2017.

Evershed, N. and Liu, R. (2016), 'The "Feral" Senate: How often do the crossbenchers actually vote against the government', *The Guardian Datablog* (online), March 15, <https://www.theguardian.com/australia-news/datablog/ng-interactive/2016/mar/15/the-feral-senate-how-often-do-the-crossbenchers-actually-vote-against-the-government>.

Hawker Britton, 'How the Senate has Voted', analysis, April 2017.

Le Grand, C. and Creighton, A., 'PwC modelling reveals one nation split into haves and have nots', *The Australian*, 27 February <http://www.theaustralian.com.au/news/pwc-modelling-reveals-one-nation-split-into-haves-and-have-nots/news-story/4cefff3976f517e07e85f14d7b480a8c>.

McCrindle, M., 'Australia's Household Income and Wealth Distribution', The McCrindle Blog, 21 June 2016 <http://mccrindle.com.au/the-mccrindle-blog/australias-household-income-and-wealth-distribution>.

OECD, Glossary of Statistical Terms <https://stats.oecd.org/glossary/detail.asp?ID=2791>.

Oxfam Australia, 'An Economy for the 99%', Australian Fact Sheet, January 2017.

Sheil, C. and Stilwell, F., 'The Wealth of the Nation: Current Data on the Distribution of Wealth in Australia', Evatt Foundation, 2016.

Western Australian Electoral Commission, 2017 State Election Results.

Woods, R. 'The Australian Election Study 2016', Australian National University, 2016.

Australian Electoral Commission 2016 Federal Election Results by division and polling place for:
>South Australia
>Victoria
>Tasmania
>Queensland
>Western Australia
>ABS State and Regional Profile Statistics
>South Australia
>Victoria
>Tasmania
>Queensland
>National

ACADEMIC JOURNALS

Blyth, M. and Matthijs, M. (2017), 'Black Swans, Lame Ducks and the mystery of IPE's missing macroeconomy', 24(2) *Review of International Political Economy* 203.

Marco, D.K., Pirie, M., Au-Yeung, W., (2009), 'A history of public debt in Australia', 1 *Economic Roundup* 1.

Marr, D., 'The White Queen: One Nation and the Politics of Race', 2017, 65 *Quarterly Essay* 1.

McSwiney, J. and Cottle, D. (2017), 'Unintended Consequences: One Nation and Neoliberalism in Contemporary Australia', 79 *Journal of Australian Political Economy* 87.

Taleb, N.M. (2011), 'The Black Swan of Cairo: How Suppressing Volatility Makes the World Less Predictable and More Dangerous', 90(3) *Review of International Political Economy* 33.

CASE LAW

Re Culleton [No 2] [2017] HCA 4.

Taylor, C. and Meinshausen, M., 'Joint report to the Land Court of Queensland on "Climate Change – Emission"', submission in *Adani Mining Pty Ltd (Adani) v Land Services of Coast and Country Inc & Ors*, [2015] QLC 48.

Transcript of proceedings, *Re Culleton; Bell v Culleton* [2014] HCA Trans 289 (21 November 2016).

REPORTS, BRIEFING PAPERS, ANALYSIS

Cox, D., Lienesch, R. and Jones, R.P., 'Beyond Economics: Fears of Cultural Displacement Pushed the White Working Class to Trump', *PRRI and The Atlantic,* 9 May 2017.

Daley, J., Wood, D. and Chivers, C. 'Regional Patterns of Australia's economy and population' (Working Paper, No 2017-8, Grattan Institute, August 2017).

Denniss, R., 'The use and abuse of economic modelling in Australia: Users' guide to tricks of the trade' (Technical Brief No 12., The Australia Institute, January 2012).

Dorling, P., 'Pauline Hanson's "neo-Austrian" economic brain: One nation hires an "anarcho-capitalist" advisor' (Report, The Australia Institute, 23 February 2017).

Dorling, P. and Richardson, R., 'Easytax resurrected: A look at One Nation's economic and taxation policies' (Report, The Australia Institute, 8 March 2017).

Jones, K., 'The Rise of an Australian Working Underclass' (Research Paper, CFMEU, September 2016).

Milanovic, B., 'Global Income Inequality by the Numbers in History and Now: An Overview' (Working Paper, No 6259, The World Bank, November 2012).

Richardson, D. and Denniss, R., 'Income and Wealth Inequality in Australia' (Policy Brief No 64, The Australia Institute, July 2014).

HANSARD, INQUIRY REPORTS AND OTHER PARLIAMENTARY MATERIALS

Commonwealth, Parliamentary Debates, Senate, 22 March 2017, 38 (Senator Brian Burston).

Commonwealth, Parliamentary Debates, Senate, 15 June 2017, (Senator Malcolm Roberts).

Commonwealth, Parliamentary Debates, Senate, 21 June 2017, 11 (Senator Pauline Hanson).

Evidence to Finance and Public Administration Committee, Legislation Committee, Senate Estimates, Parliament of Australia, Canberra, 25 May 2017 (Senator Ryan).

Grantham Floods Commission of Inquiry Report, Parliament of Queensland, October 2015.

Joint Standing Committee on Electoral Matters, Parliament of Australia, *Interim report on the inquiry into the conduct of the 2013 Federal Election: Senate Voting Practices* (2014).

Pauline Hanson's One Nation, Aged Care and The Disabled Policy, political party documents, released 29 September 1998.

SPEECHES

Lowe, P., 'Household Debt, Housing Prices and Resilience' (Text of speech delivered to the Economic Society of Australia (Qld) Business Lunch, Brisbane, 4 May 2017).

Roberts, M., 'Industrial Relations Speech to Australian Industry Group' (Text of speech delivered to Australian Industry Group, Canberra, 1 May 2017) <https://www.facebook.com/malcolmrobertsonenation/posts/1082657131878166>.

WRITTEN CORRESPONDENCE

Copy of email from Peter Gargan, 10 November 2016.

Letter from Rodney Culleton to Senator Stephen Parry, President of the Senate, 4 January 2016.

Letter from Rodney Culleton to 'Fellow Senators', 6 January 2017.

Letter from Rodney Culleton to 'Governor General' (undated).

VIDEO AND AUDIO

Cassidy, B., 'Pauline Hanson joins *Insiders*', *The ABC* (online), 5 February 2017 <http://www.abc.net.au/insiders/content/2016/s4630647.htm>.

liverpoollslsj [Liverpool School of Law and Social Justice], 'Professor Michael Dougan assesses the UK's position following vote to leave the EU', 30 June 2016 <https://www.youtube.com/watch?v=0dosmKwrAbI>.

Pauline Hanson's Please Explain, 'Pauline Hanson calls Donald Trump's Historic Election Victory: Livestream Replay', 15 January 2017 <https://www.youtube.com/watch?v=soKgD7QoJ1E>.

Phone call between One Nation Leader Pauline Hanson and former Treasurer Ian Nelson, (Published on Soundcloud), *ABC News*, June 2017 <https://soundcloud.com/abcnews/phone-call-between-one-nation-leader-pauline-hanson-and-former-treasurer-ian-nelson/s-sxue3>.

Secret One Nation Tapes, (Published on Soundcloud) *Australian Financial Review*, June 2017 <https://soundcloud.com/australianfinancialreview/secret-one-nation-tapes>.

Watson Institute for International and Public Affairs, 'Mark Blyth – Global Trumpism', 29 September 2016 <https://www.youtube.com/watch?v=Bkm2Vfj42FY>.

MISCELLANEOUS

Hanson, P., 'Senator Pauline Hanson Slams Soft Xenophon', (press release, 19 October 2016).

Roberts, M., 'Executive CV' (resume, undated).

Roberts, M., 'CSIROh!', self-published manuscript (online) 4 February 2013 <http://www.climate.conscious.com.au/CSIROh!.html>.

Acknowledgements

WRITING A BOOK IS NOT SOMETHING YOU DO ALONE. A BOOK takes many hands to make and this one is no different.

This book could not exist without the help of those named within who patiently answered my questions and shared their stories, those who couldn't be named for obvious reasons and those who showed me their homes, their towns and their cities.

To you all, I extend my deepest thanks and gratitude.

And before anyone else, I must thank Jennifer. I logged a lot of hours chasing this book and you were there through it all.

I'm fairly certain I was a rubbish media advisor, so thank you to Nick Xenophon for putting up with me and for finding time to contribute to this book. Likewise, thank you to Tony Windsor, Ricky and Kerrie-Anne Muir, and Bob Katter, whose direct contributions helped immensely.

I also owe a debt of gratitude to those with whom I shared a trench during my brief time in politics. Thank you Jono, Rex, Karina, Connie and Pat for your help and guidance, and especially to the EO staff who made it so hard to leave: Jess, Morgan and Michael, Chloe, Alex, Anna, Hayley and SB.

Some of the work that appears in this book was published originally by *Vice* and the BBC. As always, my thanks go to Julian and Madison for saving me from myself.

Thank you to Professor Peter Whiteford for help on some of those numbers, to Mark Egelstaff for letting me pick his brain, and thank you to Pas for your help on the ground. I would also like to thank Gideon Haigh who read a version of this manuscript and served as a sounding board.

Thank you to Sophie, Tom, Claire, Anna and the whole team at Hachette Australia for bringing another book into existence.

Thank you to my lawyer and friend Russell, and to my friends Shane, Sam, Tanya, Issy, Mark, Nicola, Ali and Matthew, who endured my endless monologue about the fate of the world, in part, or in full. Thank you to Michael and Georgi (I hope the little one is still okay) for giving me somewhere to stay in Melbourne, to Connor for trusting me with his car, to Sean and Ellie for putting me up in Brisbane, to Fiona for taking me out west and to Kanchana for giving the view from the mountaintop.

Thank you to the reporters of *The Age*, the *Sydney Morning Herald*, the *Saturday Paper*, *The Guardian*, *The Monthly*, The Conversation, Junkee, the ABC and *The Advertiser* whose work I have relied upon to reconstruct events and timelines.

Please don't hold it against me if I have left you off this list, it's been a long road.